Eye on Editing 2

Developing Editing Skills for Writing

Joyce S. Cain

Longman

Eye on Editing 2

Pearson Education, 10 Bank Street, White Plains, NY 10606

Vice president, director of publishing: Allen Ascher
Acquisitions editor: Laura Le Dréan
Development director: Penny Laporte
Development editor: Stacey Hunter
Vice president, director of design and production: Rhea Banker
Executive managing editor: Linda Moser
Production manager: Ray Keating
Associate production editor: Corrie Sublett-Berríos
Director of manufacturing: Patrice Fraccio
Senior manufacturing buyer: Edith Pullman
Cover design: Pat Wosczyk
Cover art: Dennis Harms
Text design: Pat Wosczyk
Text composition: TSI Graphics
Text font: 11/13 Minion
Text art: Dennis Harms
Text credits: For permission to use the selections reprinted in this book, the author is grateful to the following publishers and copyright holders:

Pages 108–109, "Men, Women Differ in Storing of Emotional Memories." Reprinted with permission of UC Irvine Communications, 2001. Tom Vasich, January 31, 2001. Pages 109–110, *OMNI Magazine*, "Psychic Pooch," by Sherry Baker, July 1990, p. 28. Pages 110–111, "Blue Wonder," © 2001, David George Gordon. Pages 111–113, "Latin American Film Explosion." Reprinted with the permission of the *New University.* Frank Morales, April 10, 2000. Pages 113–115, "Depot of Dreams," *Westways Magazine,* March/April 2001. All rights retained by the author. Copyright Amy Gerstler 2001. Pages 115–116, "Get on the Piano," *OC Family Magazine,* May 1999. Published with the permission of Churm Publishing, Inc. Pages 116–118, "Feng Shui Rearranges Your Qi." Reprinted by permission of the *New University.* Melinda Sheckells, January 15, 2001. Pages 118–121, "Excuses Don't Make the Grade." Reprinted with the permission of Christine Baron. Pages 121–123, "A First Class Party." Reprinted by permission of the Washington Post. By Lonnae O'Neal Parker, 12/28/01.

Library of Congress Cataloging-in-Publication Data

Cain, Joyce S.
  Eye on editing 2: developing editing skills for writing / Joyce S. Cain.
    p. cm.
  ISBN 0-201-62134-7 (alk. paper)
  1. English language—Textbooks for foreign speakers.   2. English
language—Rhetoric—Problems, exercises, etc.   3. Report writing—
Problems, exercises, etc.   4. Editing—Problems, exercises, etc.   I. Title:
Eye on edition two. II. Title.

PE1128 .C254 2002
808´.042—dc21   2002022856

Printed in the United States of America
 6 7 8 9 10 11 12–CRK–12 11 10 09 08 07 06

Contents

To the Teacher

Eye on Editing 2: Developing Editing Skills for Writing is designed to meet the needs of ESL writers who have developed a high-intermediate level of fluency, yet need additional practice in areas such as the passive voice, adverb clauses, and parallel structure. This book focuses on developing self-editing skills. The concise grammar explanations and the variety of editing exercises will help students master the process of editing their own work. *Eye on Editing 2* can stand on its own or serve as a supplement to reading, writing, and grammar classes. It can also be useful as a reference guide for students.

The main goal of *Eye on Editing 2* is to provide students with tools for grammatical analysis that are easy to understand and apply to their own writing. It also aids students in the production of accurate, meaningful, and appropriate language. To this end, the grammar explanations and rules focus on those errors that are most prevalent in the writing of high-intermediate level writers, although the book is an appropriate review for students at higher levels of writing proficiency as well.

Eye on Editing 2 is not intended to be a comprehensive grammar book. Grammar topics are based on an analysis of student writing errors. Because it focuses on specific problem areas, a cross-reference to other grammar books, including *Understanding and Using English Grammar,* Third Edition; *Focus on Grammar,* High-Intermediate, Second Edition; and *Grammar Express,* has been provided to assist those who would like further grammar explanations.

FORMAT AND CONTENT

Eye on Editing 2 is composed of eleven chapters—ten chapters focus on particular areas of grammar, and a final chapter provides further practice. The first ten chapters may be used in any order, and the final chapter may be drawn on as needed.

Each of the first ten chapters is composed of four sections. The first section in each chapter is a Pretest that contains sentence items that highlight the main points covered in the chapter. The Pretest allows teachers and students to assess the student's prior knowledge of the topic. The following section, Editing Focus, includes grammar explanations. When explanations are broken into subtopics, each subtopic ends with a short, sentence-level Self Check, which enables students to verify their understanding of the subtopic before moving to the next. Charts and examples are used extensively to illustrate and visually reinforce the grammar points.

The exercises in the Editing Practice section focus on the task of editing discourse—a skill students need to apply to their own writing. The exercises move students from the sentence to the discourse level, and from more guided to less guided tasks. Exercise 1, like the Pretest, asks students to locate errors in sentence-level items. Exercises 2–4 provide paragraph-level editing practice based on adapted student writing. Exercise 2 is generally a fill-in-the-blank exercise, which requires students to supply the correct form of the given word. In Exercise 3, errors are pointed out for the student to correct. Exercise 4 asks students to locate and correct grammar errors in an unmarked piece of writing. Students are always told how many errors they must identify; however, just as they do in their own writing, they must scrutinize all sentences in order to edit the piece successfully. The exercises are appropriate for homework, in-class practice, or quizzes.

Each chapter ends with a Writing Topics section—two guided writing tasks that encourage students to produce and edit for the grammatical structure presented in the chapter. The writing topics are based on themes of current interest. These topics are designed for paragraph writing but can be used for longer essays as well.

Chapter 11 consists of paragraph-level editing exercises that are similar to those in Exercise 4 in the earlier chapters. However, it requires students to edit for more than one grammar point in each essay.

Appendix 1, "Practice with Authentic Language," contains excerpts from pieces of published writing. In these exercises, students must select the correct form from alternatives. The next nine appendices offer students a reference guide to irregular verbs, subject-verb agreement, punctuation, prepositions, phrasal verbs, problem words and phrases, using quotations, an editing log, and correction symbols. The final appendix is a grammar correlation between topics presented in *Eye on Editing 2,* as well as *Understanding and Using English Grammar,* Third Edition; *Focus on Grammar,* High-Intermediate, Second Edition; and *Grammar Express.* An answer key is also provided.

FEATURES

Eye on Editing 2 aids students in the production of accurate, meaningful, and appropriate language. It is effective in doing so because of the following features:

- Grammar topics have been selected based on an analysis of student writing errors.

- The chapters can be used to supplement reading, writing, and grammar assignments.

- With its clear, concise explanations and its appendices, the text is designed to be a useful reference guide for students.

- Each chapter begins with a Pretest that allows teachers to assess students' prior knowledge and students to assess themselves.

- Chapter explanations present general grammar rules but also focus on those areas that present the most problems for student writers, providing students with specific errors to edit in their own writing.

- The exercises concentrate on the task of editing discourse—a skill that students need for their own writing development.

- The error identification required to do these exercises will carry over into students' own writing.

- All exercises are based on adapted student writing so that students are simulating the kind of editing tasks they must perform on their own writing.

- The exercises are appropriate for homework, in-class practice, or quizzes.

- The answer key facilitates independent and small group work.

- The guided writing tasks are a final comprehensive check on the editing practice students have been doing and a bridge to their own unguided writing and editing.

- The professional writing samples in Appendix 1 provide opportunities to discuss rhetorical issues.

To the Student

Eye on Editing 2 offers instruction and practice to help you become a skillful editor of your own writing. Each of the book's features was designed to assist you in accomplishing your writing goals.

GRAMMAR TOPICS: The ten chapters focus on grammar topics that are important for student writers to fully understand. By becoming aware of the potential problem spots highlighted in these chapters and how to avoid them by using the correct forms, you will eventually eliminate many errors in your own writing.

BRIEF EXPLANATIONS: The brief grammar explanations will help you reinforce your prior knowledge of particular grammar topics and help you to focus on the most important features of each topic. The charts and appendices can be used for quick reference.

STUDENT WRITING: All exercises are based on student writing. Thus, the type of editing practice that is most important for student writers is provided in the exercises in this book.

SEQUENCE OF EXERCISES: Each chapter begins with a Pretest to help you decide how much practice with a particular grammar topic you need. The following exercises become progressively more difficult as your editing skills become more proficient. At the end of each chapter, you are asked to write and edit a short piece that elicits the appropriate grammar topic.

EXTRA EDITING: When editing your own writing, it is necessary to look for more than one type of grammar error. The exercises in Chapter 11 ask you to do the same.

PUBLISHED WRITING: The Practice with Authentic Language exercises in Appendix 1 ask you to look at the writing of published authors. By studying this language, you will become aware of how particular grammatical structures are used by professional writers.

EDITING LOG: The editing log in Appendix 9 will help you become aware of the grammar errors that you make most frequently. By recording the grammar mistakes that your teacher finds in your paragraphs and essays, you will begin to see a pattern of errors. Once you know your own grammar weaknesses, you can successfully edit for and eliminate them in future writing.

Acknowledgments

Eye on Editing 2 is the result of the many valuable comments that I received from my colleagues, students, and editors. Susan Earle-Carlin, Colleen Hildebrand, and Robin Scarcella at the University of California, Irvine provided encouragement, time, and ideas that ultimately led to the final version of this book. At Pearson Education, I am especially grateful to Laura Le Dréan, whose time and countless suggestions helped guide *Eye on Editing 2* through the manuscript stage. Stacey Hunter's and Francoise Leffler's expertise during the editing process made all the difference. Without the students in the Humanities ESL Program at UCI and their feedback on exercises, this book would not exist and for that, I thank them. And again, my family and husband's undying enthusiasm and support reminded me of the importance of this long project.

Tenses and Time Shifts

PRETEST

Check your understanding of verb tenses. Put a check (✓) next to the sentences that are correct.

____ 1. Michael ran when he twisted his ankle.

____ 2. The Paris subway is efficient, clean, and safe when I was living there.

____ 3. The university has been offering this course since 1997.

____ 4. Because of all the long distance phone calls I've made this month, my phone bill will be larger than usual.

____ 5. We had seen all the videos at home, so now we have to go rent some.

____ 6. We will not be going to the lecture this evening.

____ 7. Xiao has not be feeling well for the last few weeks.

____ 8. Professor Milton is teaching at the college for many years.

____ 9. Mr. Duong will has been working here for a year by the end of next month.

____ 10. Lynda and Amy had been searching the library for an hour before they found the books they needed.

EDITING FOCUS

Knowing how to form the tenses and when to use them will help you edit your writing so that your meaning is clear. It is also important to know when to shift tenses in writing. In the following sections, you will review the form and use of the various verb tenses, as well as guidelines for using time shifts in your writing.

FORMING THE PRESENT TENSES

REGULAR VERBS IN THE SIMPLE PRESENT

The following chart shows how to form present tenses with regular verbs.

	Subject	Verb	
Simple present	I/You/We/They	love/do not love	the cold weather.
	He/She	loves/does not love	
	It	leaves/does not leave	at 5:00 P.M.
Present progressive	I	am (not) taking	
	You/We/They	are (not) taking	a long time.
	He/She/It	is (not) taking	
Present perfect	I/You/We/They	have (not) studied	French before.
	He/She	has (not) studied	
	It	has (not) rained	in the past three weeks.
Present perfect progressive	I/You/We/They	have (not) been working	for three hours.
	He/She/It	has (not) been working	

BE, HAVE, AND DO IN THE SIMPLE PRESENT

Remember that some verbs are irregular in the simple present.

Subject	Be	
I	am (not)	
He/She/It	is (not)	in the office.
They	are (not)	

Subject	*Have*	
I/You/We/They	have/do not have	enough water.
He/She/It	has/does not have	

Subject	*Do*	
I/You/We/They	do/do not do	good work.
He/She/It	does/does not do	

USING THE PRESENT TENSES

1. The simple present is used to describe or write about:
   - general truths or facts

       It takes five hours to fly from California to New York.

   - habits or routines

       Louise takes the bus to school every day.

   - books or movies

       In the novel *When I Was Puerto Rican,* **Negi moves from Puerto Rico to New York and eventually enrolls at Harvard University.**

2. The present progressive is used to describe or write about:
   - current actions or states

       Preston is studying for his test.

   - current actions over an extended time period

       Darlene is majoring in East Asian Studies.

3. The present perfect is used to describe or write about:
   - actions or events that happened at an unspecified time in the past

       They have seen that show before.

   - actions that began in the past and continue in the present

       Mrs. Alvarez has lived here since 1966.

   - recently completed actions that affect the present

       I've just finished a very difficult exam, so I'm exhausted.

4. The present perfect progressive is used to:
   - describe or write about actions that began in the past and continue up to the present

       We have been waiting for a long time.

   - emphasize the duration of an action that began in the past and has continued to the present

       We have been waiting to board the plane for two hours.

SELF CHECK 1

Correct the errors in verb tense.

1. All basketball players have been tall.

2. We haven't send your birthday present yet.

3. This semester I take four classes.

4. We are studying for the exam since last Friday.

5. Registration for classes goes on for a week as of today.

FORMING THE PAST TENSES

REGULAR VERBS IN THE SIMPLE PAST

The following chart shows how to form the different past tenses with regular verbs.

	Subject	Verb	
Simple past	I/You/He/She/We/They	cooked/did not cook	yesterday.
	It	rained/did not rain	
Past progressive	You/We/They	were (not) cooking	when it happened.
	I/He/She	was (not) cooking	
	It	was (not) raining	when we left.
Past perfect	I/You/He/She/We/They	had (not) been	to the museum before.
	It	had (not) happened	before.
Past perfect progressive	I/You/He/She/We/They	had (not) been studying	for an hour before class began.
	It	had (not) been snowing	for an hour before the plane took off.

IRREGULAR VERBS IN THE SIMPLE PAST

The verb *be* has two forms in the simple past.

Subject	Be	
I/He/She/It	was	in London.
You/We/They	were	

Some other irregular verbs are:

bring → **brought**	break → **broke**	find → **found**	have → **had**
get → **got**	go → **went**	grow → **grew**	see → **saw**

NOTE: All irregular verbs except *be* have the same past tense form for all subjects.

USING THE PAST TENSES

1. The simple past is used to describe or write about:
- actions or situations that began and ended at a specific time in the past

   Alvin graduated last June.   **Bob was sick last night.**

- habitual past actions

   We ate at this restaurant every Friday night for years.

NOTE: *Used to* or *would* are also used to refer to habitual past actions. *Used to* emphasizes a contrast with the present and is more common than *would*.

   We used to ride our bikes to school when we were children.
   I would ride my bike to school every day before I got my driver's license.

2. The past progressive is used to describe or write about:
- actions in progress at a specific time in the past

   I was studying in the library at 9:00 last night.

- past continuous actions interrupted by another action

   Lan was talking on the phone when I arrived.

- two past continuous actions happening at the same time

   While you were barbecuing the fish, I was making the salad.

3. The past perfect is used to describe or write about a past action or situation that happened or existed before another past action or time.

   In Rome, we saw the sites we had read about in our history books.

   My sister had done all the housework by noon.

NOTE: When only one past event is mentioned in a sentence, use the simple past, not the past perfect.

   We drove home in the rain last night.
   NOT
   We had driven home in the rain last night.

4. The past perfect progressive is used to describe or write about an action or event that was in progress before or until another time or event. The past perfect progressive is often used to express the duration of the first event or action.

   Celeste had been working on the project for two months when the company decided to cancel it.

SELF CHECK 2

Correct the errors in verb tense.

1. James breaked the mirror when he dropped it.

2. Connie had not been very tired last night.

3. When I saw Neha at the party, I didn't recognize her because I've never seen her before.

4. I studied when you called.

5. The sun had been shine for several hours before it started to rain.

FORMING THE FUTURE TENSES

	Subject	Verb	
Simple future	I/You/He/She/We/They	will (not) call	later today.
	It	will (not) arrive	
be going to	I	am (not) going to move	next summer.
	You/We/They	are (not) going to move	
	He/She/It	is (not) going to move	
Future progressive	I/You/He/She/It/We/They	will (not) be leaving	tomorrow.
Future perfect	I/You/He/She/It/We/They	will (not) have left	by five o'clock.
Future perfect progressive	I/You/He/She/It/We/They	will (not) have been working	for several hours by ten o'clock.

USING THE FUTURE TENSES

1. The simple future is used to describe or write about actions, events, or states that will occur in the future, including:
   - scheduled events

        The movie will begin at 8:30.

   - predictions

        Will it be sunny tomorrow? It probably will be.

   - promises

        I will never tell your secret.

   - offers

        I will drive you to school tomorrow.

        NOTE: In speech *will* is often contracted when used for offers.

            I'll drive you to school tomorrow.

   - decisions made at the moment of speaking

        I think I'll take a walk.

2. *Be going to* + verb is used to describe or write about:
   - Planned events

        We're going to work at a restaurant this summer.
        I am going to take five classes next semester.

   - predictions

        I think this class is going to be my favorite one.

3. The future progressive is used to describe or write about an action that will be in progress at a time in the future.

        John and Kim will be sailing on the lake all day Saturday.

4. The future perfect is used to describe or write about a future action that will happen before another future action or time.

        You will probably have left for the party by the time John arrives.

5. The future perfect progressive is used to describe or write about future events or actions that continue up to another future event or time. The future perfect progressive is often used to express the duration of the first event or action.

        By the time you graduate, I will have been working for several years.

6. In addition to the simple future, the simple present can be used to describe or write about scheduled events.

> **The bus departs at 6:00 tomorrow morning.**
> **The performance begins at 8:00 tonight.**

NOTE: Verbs commonly used in the simple present to refer to the future are: *arrive, begin, depart, finish, leave,* and *start.*

7. The present progressive can be used to describe or write about a previously arranged future action.

> **We're leaving town tomorrow afternoon.**

SELF CHECK 3

Correct the errors in verb tense.

1. Tomas and Ruben going to leave for Mexico tomorrow morning.

2. Zach is a year old by next summer.

3. Ria will have worn a formal gown to the birthday party next weekend.

4. The final exam tomorrow is difficult.

5. We will remodeling our house later this year.

CHOOSING THE CORRECT VERB TENSE

As a writer, it is important that you choose the verb tense that most clearly conveys your meaning. Being aware of the differences in meaning of verb tenses will help you choose the most appropriate tense. The following are verb tenses that are often confused.

PRESENT TENSES

All three of the following sentences use present time tenses, but each one conveys a different meaning.

Joleen works at the bookstore.	The simple present emphasizes the fact that the action is a habit or happens regularly; for example, *every Tuesday.*
Joleen is working at the bookstore.	The present progressive emphasizes that the action is currently happening at the time of writing, or for a temporary period of time; for example, *this week.*
Joleen has worked at the bookstore since last summer.	The present perfect emphasizes the period of time over which the event has occurred (*from last summer to the present*).

SIMPLE PAST VERSUS PRESENT PERFECT

Choose carefully between the simple past and present perfect.

I saw the movie a few months ago.	The simple past is used to describe an action that occurred at a specific time in the past.
I've seen the movie, so I think I'll stay home.	The present perfect is used for an action that occurred at an unspecified time in the past.

SIMPLE PAST VERSUS PAST PROGRESSIVE

Choose carefully between the simple past and past progressive.

I slept well last night.	The simple past is used to describe an action that occurred at a specific time in the past.
I was sleeping when she called.	The past progressive is used to describe an action that was happening in the past and was interrupted by a second action. The second action is in the simple past tense.

SIMPLE PAST VERSUS PAST PERFECT

Choose carefully between the simple past and past perfect.

He cleaned the apartment when his mother arrived.	The simple past tells us that he began cleaning when his mother arrived.
He had cleaned the apartment when his mother arrived.	The past perfect tells us that the cleaning was completed before his mother arrived.

PRESENT PERFECT VERSUS PRESENT PERFECT PROGRESSIVE

Choose carefully between the present perfect and the present perfect progressive.

Quincy has read the book.	The present perfect shows that the action has happened in the past one or more times.
Quincy has been reading the book.	The present perfect progressive emphasizes that the action is continuous and that it has not finished.

Stative Verbs

- Some verbs have stative meanings. They describe states or situations that exist. These verbs are not usually used in the progressive tenses.

    Gerald knows most of the answers on the test.

    Other verbs with stative meanings include the following:

appreciate	exist	mind	prefer
believe	fear	need	realize
belong	hate	owe	recognize
care	like	own	understand
dislike	love	please	want

- Some verbs may have a stative meaning as well as a progressive meaning.

    Gerald weighs 100 pounds. The simple present describes Gerald's state—there is no action.

    Gerald is weighing himself on the scale. The present progressive describes the action of standing on the scale and reading it.

    Other verbs that can have both stative and progressive meanings include the following:

appear	forget	include	see
be	have	look	taste
feel	imagine	remember	think

NOTE: Do not confuse a verb's stative meaning with its progressive meaning.

Paula was **tasting** the sauce while Andrew cooked the pasta.
(This refers to Paula's action of putting the sauce in her mouth and judging the flavor.)
NOT
The sauce was tasting good.
(The sauce cannot perform the action of tasting.)
BUT
The sauce **tasted** good.
(The simple past describes the sauce's state—there is no action.)

Self Check 4

Correct the errors in verb tense.

1. George has been performing in the choir once.

2. They are belonging to the Latin Club.

3. The classroom was feeling very hot during the exam.

4. She has finished the project yesterday.

5. I feel sick; I had a stomachache for an hour. I think I'll leave work early today.

USING TIME SHIFTS

Writers often shift between present, past, and future time within a piece of writing. It is important that you use verb tenses correctly in order for your reader to understand when actions and events take place.

1. Remember that when you use a time word or phrase (*tomorrow, yesterday,* or *next month*), the verb tense must correspond to it. When time is not directly mentioned, think carefully about the time you want to express, and choose the correct tense.

2. Avoid unnecessary shifts in tense, but be aware that you will often need to use several different tenses in a piece of writing. The example paragraph below shows time shifts that are necessary in order for the writer to discuss the current situation and how it relates to past and future events. Notice how the verb tenses correspond to the related time words or phrases.

> (1) ***This year*** the history department **requires** students with a major in history to take a new four-credit-hour seminar in their junior year. (2) This **means** that students must now take a minimum of forty credit hours in history courses to graduate. (3) ***In previous years,*** the minimum **was** thirty-six credit hours. (4) The department **will review** the program ***after two academic years. Then*** the department **will decide** whether or not it **will keep** this new requirement.

NOTE: In this paragraph, the boldfaced verbs show a shift from the present to the past to the future. The writer shifts from a discussion of what is true in the present (*this year*), to what was true in the past (*previous years*), and finally, to what will happen in the future (*after two academic years*). Shifting tenses is necessary to compare the situation now and in the past, and to explain how it may change in the future.

> **TIP**
> Pay close attention to time shifts when you read for school or for pleasure. Notice how time words or phrases signal these shifts in time.

SELF CHECK 5

In the following paragraph, the underlined verbs are not correct. Write the correct verb form above each underlined verb.

Last year we (1) <u>spend</u> our vacation in the Caribbean. We relaxed under the sun and sipped our drinks as the ocean breezes cooled us. This summer we (2) <u>drive</u> to the mountains to spend our vacation in a house on a lake. We (3) <u>planned</u> to stay there for one week. Next year we will have more time for our vacation, so we (4) <u>consider</u> going somewhere farther away. Perhaps we (5) <u>are going</u> to Europe.

EDITING PRACTICE

1 *Put a check (✓) next to the sentences that use verb tenses and time shifts correctly. Correct the sentences that have errors.*

____ 1. Many people are believing that increased security has led to a loss of freedom.

____ 2. We hope that there will be more music classes next semester.

____ 3. My seven-year-old son has read the first Harry Potter book last week.

____ 4. They put the special glasses on so that they could see the movie in 3D.

____ 5. I think it is raining tomorrow.

____ 6. When we got to the party, our whole family was there.

____ 7. Professor Xu was finishing his final lecture when the room erupted in applause.

____ 8. According to the class schedule, we will have been writing a paper every week of the term.

____ 9. By the time the semester ends, the class will have learned to write strong thesis statements and good topic sentences.

____ 10. The Whaling Museum will been showing a film on the whale ship *The Essex* for the next two weeks.

____ 11. Virginia and Louis have been dating for two years.

____ 12. She reads that book four times so far.

2 *Read the following paragraph. Complete the paragraph with the correct form of the verb.*

Of the many forms of self-improvement that people are experimenting with, exercise seems to be the most popular. Forms of exercise that involve relaxation such as yoga, tai chi, and meditation _____ popular recently. One relaxing exercise that isn't discussed a
1. become / have become
lot, but one that I find especially beneficial, is fishing. It is more physical than most people

_____ aware of, but it is also very calming like yoga, tai chi, and meditation. I started fishing
2. were / are
with my dad when I was a child, and I _____ ever since. Before I
3. have been fishing / fished
_____ big enough to hold a reel, I had gone out on the water with my dad many
4. was / had been
times. When I was old enough to fish, I started fishing with my father. Back then I

_____ to come home with the biggest fish and the most fish, but now I
5. used to like / would to like
_____ more satisfaction in the act of fishing than in the result. Throughout time, many
6. find / found
fishermen _____ fishing as a form of self-improvement. While fishermen
7. see / have seen

_____ for the "big one," they have nothing but time to think and to relax.

8. waited / are waiting

Isn't that the goal of many forms of self-improvement? Over the years, the times I

_____ fishing with my dad, friends, and even by myself are too

9. have been spending / have spent

precious to forget. Another wonderful part of fishing is that a person is never too old to do it, so I

_____ for as long as I live.

10. am going to fish / fish

3 *In the following paragraph, the underlined verbs are not correct. Write the correct verb form above each underlined verb.*

Rage is an emotion that is felt everywhere and by people of all ages. It is one feeling that

(1) <u>was</u> very hard to ignore. No matter how hard one tries to repress rage, it (2) <u>has still surfaced</u>.

We may see rage in the form of insulting words or violent actions. A common form of rage that

we (3) <u>hear</u> about over the past several years is road rage. Many people (4) <u>entered</u> the roadways to

find drivers yelling at each other over small accidents or during traffic jams. People (5) <u>are seeming</u>

to have quick tempers when it comes to small frustrations. Themes of rage have even shown up in

modern literature. In the short story "Like a Winding Sheet" by Ann Petry, Mr. Johnson represses

the rage he feels toward his female boss because he cannot "bring himself to hit a woman." He

(6) <u>took</u> the insults from his boss and the imagined insults from a coffee shop waitress, and these

insults turn to rage inside him. He (7) <u>is arriving</u> at home and immediately takes his rage out on

his wife. This story (8) <u>has ended</u> tragically, and sadly, similar consequences of rage (9) <u>became</u>

more and more frequent in real life. It's an emotion that we should be aware of and teach our

children to control; otherwise, we, our children, and our children's children (10) <u>experience</u> many

frightening and unnecessary consequences of rage.

4 *The following paragraph has ten errors in the use of verb tenses. Find and correct the errors.*

It seems that many teenagers looked at driving as a right rather than as a privilege that

they are having to earn. In order for these young adults to take this privilege more seriously, many

states recently change their laws so that it is harder for teens to be on the road. I believe this is

important because I have saw many dangerous incidents involving teenage drivers since I had

gotten my license five years ago. I know that I was part of the problem when I was a new driver, and I am in many near accidents due to my careless driving. However, I was lucky. In order to keep everyone safe on the road, I think that parents and lawmakers should prohibit people below the age of eighteen from driving at night, with friends, and on the freeways. Most unsafe driving seemed to occur when one of these factors is present. To make the restrictions easier on teens, some cities have been consider improving their public transportation systems. Though it will have been difficult for rural areas with small populations to expand public transportation, the benefits will be worth the cost. Changes in laws and improvements in public transportation could make a difference in keeping drivers safe. These changes may make teenage drivers mad at first, but if the changes are implemented, everyone is more safe in the future.

WRITING TOPICS

Choose one of the topics below, and write at least one paragraph. Think carefully about the verb tenses you choose and the time shifts you make. After you complete your first draft, concentrate on editing your work. Keep in mind the editing practice from this chapter.

1. Throughout life, people set goals for themselves that they sometimes achieve and other times do not. Describe the goals you have had in the past and the goals you currently have. Which goals have you achieved and why? What could someone learn about you by knowing the goals you have set for yourself?

2. As weather predictions become more accurate, people are better able to prepare for bad weather such as hurricanes, blizzards, and tornados. Describe what people do in an area of the world you are familiar with when bad weather is approaching. What did they do in the past that was helpful or not helpful, and what can they do now to avoid disasters associated with the weather?

Go to pages 102 and 104 for more practice with verb tenses and time shifts.

CHAPTER 2

Modals

PRETEST

Check your understanding of modals. Put a check (✓) next to the sentences that are correct.

____ 1. Julie must have fixed the computer because it is working now.

____ 2. Christopher could of finished sooner in the triathlon, but he isn't a very strong swimmer.

____ 3. Jason can to write a good essay if he works hard.

____ 4. Criminology majors usually find jobs within the justice system, but they might have found jobs in education, too.

____ 5. They had better meet the next deadline on their project.

____ 6. Justine should study last night, but she went to the movies instead.

____ 7. Family possessions may have special significance to some and have no significance to others.

____ 8. May you tell me the time?

____ 9. We were supposed to have studied before we went out for the evening.

____ 10. Medical interns can practice not until they get their licenses.

EDITING FOCUS

Modals such as *should, would,* and *must,* and phrasal modals such as *be able to, be supposed to,* and *have to* are used in both present/future tenses and in past tenses to express ideas like ability, necessity, or possibility. As a writer and editor, you need to be able to form and use modals correctly.

FORMING MODALS

PRESENT/FUTURE

1. Use modal + base form of the verb to form the present or future of modals.

   Mark **can read** Russian.

   Drivers **must wear** seatbelts at all times.

2. For negatives, use modal + *not* + base form of the verb.

   Mark **cannot read** Spanish.

   Simon **should not walk** into class late.

   NOTE: Modals do not have different forms for different subjects and are never followed by *to*.

   Jill **could drive** him to school.
   NOT
   Jill *coulds drive* him to school.
   Brandon **should arrive** after everyone else.
   NOT
   Brandon *should to arrive* after everyone else.

PRESENT PROGRESSIVE

1. Use modal + *be* + present participle (*-ing*) to form the present progressive of modals.
   Yolanda **should be studying** now.

2. Use modal + *not* + *be* + present participle to form the negative present progressive.
   Howard **may not be taking** the train today.

PAST

1. Use modal + *have* + past participle to form the past of most modals.
   I **should have stayed** home last night.

   We **should have drunk** more water before yesterday's hike.

2. Use modal + *not* + *have* + past participle to form the negative past tense of modals.

> **Marty may not have gotten an A on the last exam.**

> **I should not have skipped class yesterday.**

TIP

In spoken English, the contraction for *have* sounds like the preposition *of.* Don't confuse the two in your writing.

He could've been a doctor.
NOT
He could of been a doctor.

---

3. When it shows ability, the past of *can* is *could.*

> **Dr. McManus can speak two languages fluently now.**

> **As a child, Dr. McManus could speak three languages fluently.**

4. To form the past tense of phrasal modals (e.g., *be able to, be supposed to, have to*), use the past tense of the verbs *be* and *have.* These verbs must agree with their subjects.

> **We were able to see / were not able to see the city lights as the plane flew over San Francisco.**

> **The doctor said Esther was supposed to run / was not supposed to run in gym class today.**

> **Donald and Di had to work / didn't have to work this morning.**

SELF CHECK 1

Correct the errors in the formation of modals.

1. William should of traveled with us last summer.

2. Andrea should be wait at the airport when you arrive.

3. Josh should have not written that letter to his girlfriend.

4. Robin and Megan could played the piano when they were young.

5. Norman had not to work yesterday because it was a holiday.

USING MODALS

Meaning	Present	Future	Past
Showing Ability	can be able to I **can** lift fifty pounds. She **is able** to run a marathon. She **will be able** to come. Last year I **could** lift 100 pounds. She **wasn't able** to come.	will be able to	could was/were able to
Making Requests	can could would **Can** you help me? **Can** you help me next week?	can could would	
Showing Possibility	can may might could He **might** change his major. We **may** leave tomorrow. I **could have** left early, but I didn't.	can may might could	may have might have could have
Showing Near Certainty *(deduction)*	must John looks awful; he **must** be sick. It **must have** rained. The ground is wet.		must have
Asking For and Giving Permission	can could may **May** I ask you a question? You **may** use my car on Saturday.	can could may	
Showing Necessity	must have to Do you **have to** work right now? Do you **have to** work tomorrow? She **had to** take the medicine.	must have to	had to

(continued page 19)

Meaning	Present	Future	Past
Showing Prohibition	must not cannot You **cannot** turn right at this intersection. They **must not** do that next semester.	must not cannot	
Showing Lack of Necessity	do not + have to You **do not have to** take the exam. We **will not have** to go next time. They **did not have to** answer the question.	do not + have to	did not + have to
Giving Advice/ Making Suggestions	had better (not) should ought to could can We **had better** leave early tomorrow. She **ought to have** taken drawing lessons. You **can** borrow that book from the library.	had better (not) should ought to could can	had better (not) have should have ought to have could have
Showing Expectation	be supposed to We **are supposed to** be in class right now. You **are supposed to** study tonight. You **were supposed to have** left yesterday.	be supposed to	was/were supposed to have
Showing Preference	would rather John **would rather** write an essay than take a test. Kim **would rather** start school next fall than next spring. He **would rather have** eaten dessert first.	would rather	would rather have
Repeated Past Action			would
	When he was younger, he **would** read the same book over and over again.		

SELF CHECK 2

Correct the errors in modal use.

1. Since the surgery, he doesn't have to eat fatty foods like french fries.

2. Andrea wasn't here last night, but she may have been because we had a good time.

3. May you call me at home tonight?

4. We're not sure where they went last night, but they would have been at the movies.

5. The final project was due at 8:00 yesterday morning. I must have completed it to pass the class.

EDITING PRACTICE

1 *Put a check (✓) next to the sentences that form and use modals correctly. Correct the sentences that have errors.*

___ 1. You must have calcium in your diet to have strong bones.

___ 2. Coach Arnold should have been a fast swimmer since she was in the Olympics.

___ 3. They closed all the shutters so they could have seen the movie better.

___ 4. Elbert got an A on the exam. He must have stayed up all night studying.

___ 5. Paul can fixes anything in the house.

___ 6. Writing my term paper should have took less time than it actually did.

___ 7. You will receive a B on the exam in order to pass the course.

___ 8. Jenna had to buy a new car because her old one broke down so often.

___ 9. Shinna was suppose to teach in Japan last summer, but he didn't.

___ 10. We ought to have listened to our parents more often.

2 *Read the following paragraph. Choose the modal that best completes each sentence, and write it on the line.*

In addition to formal schooling, team sports _____ one of the best

1. may be / may have been

ways for children to learn cooperation, teamwork, and the importance of following directions.

Very few activities mirror the cooperation that is needed in the workplace as well as team sports.

When children are on a team, they _____ to listen to directions, carry out

2. had / have

their individual roles, and try not to blame others when things don't work according to plan.

Children _____ with others before playing sports, and they

3. may not work / may not have worked

_____ the importance of sharing. Although parents

4. may not learn / may not have learned

_____ these skills at home, children _____ carefully

5. may teach / would teach   **6. might not listen / should not listen**

until their peers and a coach are involved. The only drawback to team sports _____

7. should be / can be

the parents. Everyone has heard the stories of angry, out-of-control parents at their children's

sporting events. Perhaps these parents _____ playing group sports

8. should begin / are supposed to begin

themselves, so that they _____ the same lessons of teamwork and

9. ought to learn / can learn

cooperation that their children are learning.

---

3 *In the following paragraph, the underlined modal and verb combinations are not correct. Write the correct modal above each underlined modal-verb combination. There may be more than one way to correct the errors.*

There is an old Chinese fable about good luck and bad luck. The story begins with an old farmer who lost his only horse. All the other farmers in his village **(1)** <u>must feel</u> horrible for him because all they **(2)** <u>could have talked</u> about was his stroke of bad luck. However, all the old farmer could say was, "Good luck, bad luck, who knows?" A few days later, the runaway horse returned with two wild horses following it. The farmers in the village **(3)** <u>had better be</u> jealous because they only spoke of the old farmer's good luck. The old farmer simply responded, "Good luck, bad luck, who knows?" While the old farmer's son was trying to tame the two new wild horses, he broke his leg, and the other farmers were saddened by the old farmer's recurring bad luck. All the old farmer **(4)** <u>might say</u> was, "Good luck, bad luck, who knows?" Several days later, the emperor's soldiers marched through the village taking all able-bodied men and boys to fight in the emperor's war. The old farmer's son was left behind because of his broken leg. The villagers found the old farmer's luck to once again be good, but all the old farmer **(5)** <u>would have said</u> was, "Good luck, bad luck, who knows?"

The concept of good luck and bad luck might be alluring to many, but the old farmer in the Chinese fable seems to have the best attitude toward both kinds of luck. We **(6)** <u>must have</u> good luck one day, but the next day that good luck **(7)** <u>would turn</u> to bad. The old farmer is probably telling us that we **(8)** <u>should not have taken</u> luck too seriously, and that we should try to make the best of both good and bad without relying on the concept of luck.

4 *The following paragraph has ten errors in the use of modals. Find and correct the errors.*

Many believe that a single event can change the course of someone's life. The event should be large or small, but it can make such an impact that one's life is never the same again. This happened to Daniel Rudy Rutteiger, whose life story is told in the film *Rudy.* Rudy dreams of going to the University of Notre Dame and playing football, but Rudy is small and not highly academic, so his friends and family think he will has to be satisfied as a steel worker like his father and his brothers. For years, Rudy puts aside his dream and works in the steel plant, until his best friend is killed in an industrial accident. Rudy reclaims his dream and goes to Notre Dame to play football. Rudy will never have gone to Notre Dame, played football there, and been the subject of a major motion picture if this one life-changing event had not happened. Other people's lives must not change as dramatically as Rudy's, but events such as learning to swim, learning a foreign language, or even learning to ride a motorcycle could have impacted life in unforeseen ways.

Like Rudy, I am able to begin college last fall. This was because of a move my parents made. At the time of the move, I didn't realize how different my life in the United States will be because of this one event. I have to speak two languages, own my own car, and work in any field I choose due to this single event. I don't think most of us realize the importance that one choice must make in life, but like Rudy's and my experiences show, one event ought to make all the difference in the world.

WRITING TOPICS

Choose one of the topics below, and write at least one paragraph. Use a variety of modals. After you complete your first draft, concentrate on editing your work. Keep in mind the editing practice from this chapter.

1. Everyone makes mistakes in life. Describe a time when you made a mistake, and explain how you could have handled the situation better than you did. What should you have done to avoid the mistake? How are you a better person today because of this event in your life?

2. How do you behave when you are asked to do something you don't want to do? How can you be honest without hurting someone's feelings? How have you handled this type of situation in the past? Should you have done something differently? If so, how would you handle it now?

Go to pages 102 and 103 for more practice with modals.

Nouns and Determiners

PRETEST

*Check your understanding of nouns and determiners. Put a check (✓)
next to the sentences that are correct.*

____ 1. Omar has a lot of confidences in himself.

____ 2. Your results are same as my results.

____ 3. He tested the three hypotheses and found that they were all
valid.

____ 4. The news on television are always bad.

____ 5. I just finished a good book that I think you would like.

____ 6. Orange has a lot of vitamin C.

____ 7. Jake has to take a trash out tonight before he leaves.

____ 8. Mr. and Mrs. Adams loved the foreign film that you
recommended.

____ 9. This book doesn't have any picture to help children understand
the story.

____ 10. Each of the assignments is worth 10 percent of the total grade.

EDITING FOCUS

The four types of determiners that are used before nouns are articles (*a, an, the*), quantifiers (*many, a little*, etc.), demonstrative adjectives (*this, that, these, those*), and possessive adjectives (*my, your, his,* etc.). Though the rules for using determiners are complex, the following general rules can help you to use most determiners correctly. When deciding which determiner to use with each noun, you need to know whether the noun is count or noncount.

NOUNS

COUNT NOUNS

1. Count nouns are nouns that have singular and plural forms. The plural is generally formed by adding –*s* or –*es*. Spelling changes are required in some cases.

   computer → computers   baby → babies

   tomato → tomatoes   leaf → leaves

2. Some count nouns have irregular plural forms.

   person → people   phenomenon → phenomena

   child → children   hypothesis → hypotheses

   man → men   syllabus → syllabi

   TIP
   Refer to a dictionary if you are not certain of a plural form.

3. Singular count nouns must always be preceded by a determiner.

   Did you finish **the** project for **your** history teacher?

   NOT
   Did you finish project for history teacher?

   There hasn't been **a** person in **the** store all day.

   NOT
   There hasn't been person in store all day.

NONCOUNT NOUNS

1. Noncount or uncountable nouns do not have plural forms and generally cannot be counted. Some examples of noncount nouns are:

   information   intelligence   love   milk   news

2. The indefinite articles *a* and *an* cannot be used with noncount nouns.

There is pollution in all parts of the world.

There is some pollution in all parts of the world.

NOT
There is a pollution in all parts of the world.

3. Many noncount nouns can be placed into categories.

Abstract nouns or concepts	adolescence, adulthood, advice, anger, behavior, confidence, courage, discrimination, diversity, education, evidence, fun, happiness, health, honesty, importance, information, knowledge, laughter, luck, news, patience, progress, proof, research, significance, time, transportation, violence, wealth
Natural materials	blood, dirt, dust, gold, ice, iron, paper, sand, silver, water
Natural occurrences	electricity, fire, fog, light, pollution, rain, smog, snow, steam, sunshine, wind
Fields of study	biology, chemistry, economics, history, literature, mathematics, medicine, physics, politics
Groups of similar items	equipment, furniture, garbage, homework, jewelry, luggage, machinery, money, scenery, traffic, vocabulary, work

NOTE: Noncount nouns use singular verbs.

Anger is a destructive emotion.

Research has revealed many causes of cancer.

4. Some nouns can be both count and noncount. Note how the meaning changes from general to more specific when the noncount noun becomes a count noun.

General liquid	Many people drink **coffee** with breakfast.
Specific serving	I'd like two small **coffees** to go, please.
General substance	The building has large windows made of **glass**.
Specific object	I dropped two **glasses** and they broke.
General food	I'll go to the store and get some **cheese**.
Specific type	The shop sells forty different **cheeses**.

TIP

If you are using a noun for the first time, always find out if the noun is count [C for countable] or noncount [U for uncountable] in a learner's dictionary, such as the *Longman Dictionary of American English.*

SELF CHECK 1

Correct the errors in count and noncount nouns. Correct the verbs if necessary.

1. Brian got a new computer equipment last night.

2. The violences in our area are getting worse every year.

3. We ordered three large tea.

4. Pam wrote essay for her English class last night.

5. Physics are my favorite subject.

ARTICLES

THE INDEFINITE ARTICLES *A* AND *AN*

1. Use *a* or *an* with singular count nouns that are not specifically identified or that express a general meaning.

   Kiren and Ivar went to a concert last night.
   (We don't know which concert. It was one of any number of concerts.)

   I had a bagel for breakfast.
   (We don't know which bagel, and it is not important to know which bagel.)

2. Use *a* or *an* with singular count nouns to make generalizations about people, objects, or concepts. A plural noun with no article conveys the same general meaning.

   A new car must have an airbag.

   OR

   New cars must have airbags.
   (All cars now have this requirement.)

3. Do not use *a* or *an* with noncount nouns.

   Amilia has bad luck in Las Vegas.

   NOT
   Amilia has a bad luck in Las Vegas.

   NOTE: *A* is used with nouns that begin with consonant sounds, while *an* is used with nouns that begin with vowel sounds.

   The textbook has a discussion section at the end of each chapter.

   There is an Appalachian folk song on the radio.

   A university student must give up some of his or her leisure time to study.
   (University begins with a consonant sound—"yuniversity.")

   It is an honor to graduate with academic recognition.
   (Honor begins with a vowel sound—"ahnor.")

THE DEFINITE ARTICLE *THE*

1. Use *the* when a noun is mentioned for the second time and your reader is familiar with it. The first time a noun is mentioned, the indefinite article *a* or *an* is generally used.

    **Yesterday Kazuo got a speeding ticket when he was driving to school. He says
    that the ticket is going to cost him $150.**

2. Use *the* with count nouns and noncount nouns to express specific meaning. The reader knows which person, object, or concept is being referred to. *The* is generally used when the noun is followed by an adjective clause or prepositional phrase, since the noun becomes specific with the description following it.

    The concert last night was excellent.
    (Both the writer and reader know which concert is being referred to.)

    The cars in our garage don't have air bags.
    (These are specific cars; they are the ones in our garage.)

    The evidence that the police found is strong.
    (This is specific evidence—the evidence the police found.)

    Do you have the instructions for the printer?
    (Both the writer and the reader know which instructions are being referred to.)

3. Use *the* with singular count nouns to refer to a type of animal, invention, or currency but not a specific one.

    The hawk is a bird of prey.

    The telephone was invented in the nineteenth century.

    The yen is the currency of Japan.

4. Use *the* after an *of* phrase that shows quantity, for example:

all of the	one of the	some of the
more of the	most of the	half of the

    I answered most of the questions on the exam.

5. Use *the* + adjective (without a noun) to refer to a group of people, for example:

the young	the old	the elderly	
the rich	the poor	the unemployed	the homeless
the sick	the injured	the disabled	the dead
the English	the Chinese	the French	

    The elderly should be respected.

    The homeless need more help from the government.

6. Use *the* with superlatives, ordinal numbers, and the adjective *same*.

    Jonah is not the best student in our class anymore.

    I liked the movie better the second time I saw it.

    Are you taking the same class as Karen?

7. Some idiomatic expressions always use the article *the.*

> Every day Ulla eats breakfast **in the morning** at 7:00 and lunch **in the afternoon** at 1:00, but she never eats dinner at night.

> We love to *go to* **the movies /the beach /the park.**

> They have to *go to* **the bank /the store /the library.**

No Article or Zero Article (Ø)

1. Use no article with plural count nouns and noncount nouns to express a general meaning, an entire class of people, objects, or concepts.

> My boyfriend's father collects **stamps.**
> *(He collects many kinds of stamps; we don't know the specific kind.)*

> My grandfather gives **advice** that is not relevant in this day and age.
> *(He gives many types of irrelevant advice. The type of advice is not specified.)*

2. Many proper nouns use no article. Do not use an article with a proper noun unless it is part of the name.

> The restaurant is on **Brookhurst** Avenue.

> **NOT**
> The restaurant is on *the Brookhurst* Avenue.

> **BUT**
> They lived in **the United States** for six years. *(part of the name)*

3. Some idiomatic expressions use no article.

> We love to **go downtown** whenever possible.

> Do you **go to school** every day?

> My father **goes to work** at 7:30 A.M. and **goes to bed** at 10:00 P.M.

> Business people always travel **by plane/bus/train/car.**

> I spend a lot of time **at college/home/work.**

Summary of Article Usage

Use the diagram to help you decide which articles to use with nouns.

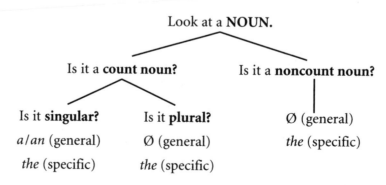

SELF CHECK 2

Correct the errors involving articles.

1. Doctor must continually update his or her medical knowledge.

2. Computer is the most important invention of the twentieth century.

3. The hawks are birds of prey.

4. I just bought my mother a gift for her birthday, but I left a gift in my car.

5. Some of homework assignments are easy.

QUANTIFIERS

Some quantifiers are only used with count nouns, others are only used with noncount nouns, and some are used with both count and noncount nouns.

QUANTIFIERS USED WITH COUNT NOUNS

	Quantifier	Count Nouns
Singular	another	another apple
	each	each student
	every	every day
	one	one test
Plural	a couple of	a couple of dollars
	both	both children
	one of the/ my/ your/ our/ etc.	one of my teachers
	each of the	each of the students
	every one of the /my /your/ our/ etc.	every one of the essays
	(not) many/too many	not many/too many people
	many of the	many of the colleges
	a few	a few friends
	(very) few	very few people
	several/a number of	several/a number of classes
	a large number of	a large number of cars
	two/three	two/three days

QUANTIFIERS USED WITH NONCOUNT NOUNS

Quantifier	Noncount Nouns
a little	a little salt
(not) much	not much time
too much	too much water
(very) little	very little sun
a great deal of	a great deal of love
a large amount of	a large amount of rain
a bit of	a bit of sugar

QUANTIFIERS USED WITH COUNT AND NONCOUNT NOUNS

Quantifier	Count Nouns	Noncount Nouns
all	all students	all knowledge
a lot of	a lot of books	a lot of progress
lots of	lots of classes	lots of patience
some	some days	some rain
any	any magazines	any luck
most	most workers	most advice
no	no children	no information
plenty of	plenty of hypotheses	plenty of research
(the) other	the other car	the other luggage

NOTE: There is a difference between *few* and *a few* and *little* and *a little*. *A few* means several and gives a positive meaning. *Few* means almost none.

> **We still have a few opportunities to improve our grades.**
> *(There is still a good chance to improve our grades.)*

> **We have few opportunities to improve our grades.**
> *(There isn't much chance to improve our grades.)*

A little means some and gives a positive meaning. *Little* means almost none or not enough.

> **Raymond's parents give him a little money for his tuition.**
> *(They give him some, or a small amount of money.)*

> **Raymond's parents give him little money for his tuition.**
> *(They don't give him enough money.)*

UNITS OF MEASURE USED WITH NONCOUNT NOUNS

Units of measure are used with noncount nouns. The units are countable.

a piece of candy	two **pieces** of candy
a glass of milk	two **glasses** of milk
an ounce of water	eight **ounces** of water
a gallon of gas	ten **gallons** of gas
a pair of pants	two **pairs** of pants

Did you put gas in the car?   **Yes, I bought fifteen gallons of gas.**

Brice loves chocolate.   **In fact, he just ate four pieces of chocolate.**

SELF CHECK 3

Correct the errors in quantifiers.

1. Parents treat their children similarly in every cultures.

2. The professor gave us few information about tomorrow's exam.

3. André is very popular at school, but he only invited a little friends to his party.

4. The recipe calls for six ounce of milk.

5. Our professor gave us too much papers to write this semester.

DEMONSTRATIVE AND POSSESSIVE ADJECTIVES

DEMONSTRATIVE ADJECTIVES

1. The demonstrative adjectives are *this, that, these,* and *those. This* and *that* are used with a singular count noun or noncount noun and *these* and *those* with a plural noun.

    This house has three bedrooms.

    That vocabulary is very difficult to remember.

    Let's take those magazines to the library.

2. Demonstrative adjectives show the contrast between near and far. *This* and *these* refer to people, objects, or concepts that are close by or that were recently discussed, while *that* and *those* refer to people, objects, or concepts that are at some distance or that were discussed in the past.

    I took analytic geometry last year. That class was the hardest one I have ever taken.
    (*The class was taken a year ago, so "that" is used to indicate the class's distance from the present.*)

    I didn't understand yesterday's lecture, and these notes don't make any sense to me.
    (*The notes were taken recently and are possibly in the speaker's hands as he or she speaks. "These" indicates close proximity.*)

POSSESSIVE ADJECTIVES

1. The possessive adjectives are *my, your, his, her, its, one's, our,* and *their.* They can be used with singular or plural nouns.

   My room is on the fifth floor of the dorm.

   The host sat his guests around the dining room table.

   Do you know much about their research?

2. *One* means any person or people in general. The use of *one* and the possessive *one's* is impersonal and very formal. It is less commonly used than impersonal *you* and *your.*

   One should take care of one's health.

   You should take care of your health. *(more common)*

   NOTE: *One's* shows possession and is not the contraction for *one is.*

   It is important to take care of one's health.

   > **TIP**
   >
   > Underline all the singular count nouns in your writing. Make sure that each one is preceded by a determiner.

SELF CHECK 4

Correct the errors involving demonstrative and possessive adjectives.

1. These grammar is easier for Carlo than for me.

2. Investment counselors recommend learning about you're retirement options early.

3. Where is there new house?

4. Do you remember the Italian movie we saw last year? This movie was the best I've ever seen.

5. Juanita bought this computer programming books over the Internet.

EDITING PRACTICE

 Put a check (✓) next to the sentences that use nouns and determiners correctly. Correct the sentences that have errors. Correct the verbs if necessary.

___ 1. Discriminations against a minority group can cause many problems.

___ 2. It is helpful to have good dictionary.

___ 3. Sebastian just got some new clothing. He bought three shirts, two belts, and a pair of pants.

___ 4. The telephone was an important invention in the late 1800s.

___ 5. Do you want to study? Let's go to library.

___ 6. Claudia just moved to a new town, but she already has few friends.

_____ 7. I don't have any money. Do you have a little dollars I can borrow?

_____ 8. One of my favorite dessert is coconut ice cream.

_____ 9. Our rival high school received largest number of awards at the academic decathalon competition.

_____ 10. All weather reports forecast snow for tomorrow.

_____ 11. Helene has three roommates, and each one has a different schedule.

_____ 12. The first witness during the trial told a lie. Because of a lie, he will have to a pay $500 fine.

2 *Complete the following paragraph with the correct nouns and determiners.*

When my teacher asked me to think about _____ truth behind _____ phrase,
                                          1. a / the   **2. that / the**

"Friends are like family," I could only recall the important role that _____ best friend Pierre
                                                                        3. my / Ø

played in my life during high school. I was a sophomore in high school when my parents decided

to move back to _____ Indonesia. At that point, I had been in _____ United States for
                 4. the / Ø   **5. the / Ø**

six years, and I felt that it was more of a home to me than Indonesia. Fortunately, Pierre and his

family agreed to let me live with them until I finished _____ high school and went off to
                                                         6. the / Ø

_____ college. Pierre and I had been good friends since junior high school when he moved
7. a / Ø

here from France. We shared _____ similar life experiences since we were both
                             8. much / many

immigrants in a new country, but it wasn't until my family moved and I lived with Pierre that

I truly understood the phrase, "friends are like family." From that point until high school

graduation, we spent more time together than apart. Every _____ of support that a
                                                           9. type / types

family usually provides was provided by my best friend and his family. We were inseparable and

most of our friends even called us "the twins." Nothing can ever replace the significance or

importance of family, but I found that _____ friends can sometimes be a very good
                                         10. Ø / the

substitute and often even better than the real thing.

3 *In the following paragraph, the underlined determiners and nouns are not correct. Write the correct determiner or noun above each underlined word or phrase.*

It seems that we hear phrases such as "he is like family to me" and "she's just like my sister" more and more often nowadays. On the one hand, **(1)** those phrases imply the closeness of family, but on the other hand, they imply the phenomenon of substituting friends for family. Are our friends taking **(2)** place of our families? The answer to **(3)** those question may be found if we look at different age groups. Family and friends hold different levels of **(4)** importances as we progress through **(5)** each stages of life. The family holds the primary place of influence during childhood, but as children reach **(6)** the adolescence, friends begin to take the place of family, and teenagers are likely to feel they are closer to **(7)** his friends than they are to their family. **(8)** These might remain true until people have children of their own or they reach old age. At these stages in life, no one can replace family, and the cycle begins again for the children. Furthermore, it is true that because of the pace and mobility of today's society, friends are taking on more **(9)** of tasks once reserved for family members. Hopefully, friends add to the depth and variety of our relationships, but never replace the important role that family has played in people's lives throughout **(10)** histories.

4 *The following paragraph has ten errors in the use of nouns or determiners. Find and correct the errors.*

One of the best aspect of my college campus is its diversity. The faculty, staff, and student come from all over the world. In fact, the faculty and students are recruited with a racial, economic, and gender balance in mind. Over the past few years, the computer science department has actively sought female faculty, and this has in turn increased the number of female students in department. Another ways the campus encourages and promotes diversities is through the classes it offers. The humanities and social science departments have several classes that educate students about a variety of cultures, religions, and literature. These classes are some of most popular on campus and fill up quickly each semesters. As on all college campuses, there are a lot of clubs and student organizations at my school. These social groups encourage students from different groups to mix and get to know each other in informal and friendly setting. A few group have cultural nights when their members present songs, dances, and food from different parts of the world. My friends and I especially enjoy tasting food from different regions. I believe that as the world gets smaller, the steps that my college campus is taking to promote diversity will help its students to understand and accept each other. Hopefully, these simple steps will make the world more peaceful place in the future.

WRITING TOPICS

Choose one of the topics below, and write at least one paragraph. Use a variety of nouns and determiners. After you complete your first draft, concentrate on editing your work. Keep in mind the editing practice from this chapter.

1. People generally consider telling lies or concealing the truth to be unethical, or wrong. However, most people do not tell the whole truth in all situations. Do you believe that deception is ever justified? If so, when do you believe that it is acceptable to tell a lie or to hide the truth? If possible, include examples to support your opinion.

2. The telephone, the car, and the computer are just a few inventions that have radically changed people's lives. Choose an important invention, and describe how life was different before the invention and how life has changed due to this invention.

Go to pages 103 and 104 for more practice with nouns and determiners.

The Passive Voice

CHAPTER 4

PRETEST

Check your understanding of the passive voice. Put a check (✓) next to the sentences that are correct.

____ 1. My favorite novel is translate from Russian.

____ 2. The photograph will be taken right before sunset.

____ 3. More cars were manufactured last year than had been manufactured the year before.

____ 4. The package should be send to his business.

____ 5. Last year the class teaches by my favorite professor in the department.

____ 6. He deserved to be rewarded for his hard work.

____ 7. New computer technology is been developed constantly.

____ 8. All the exams have been returned.

____ 9. The conference was been held at the hotel near the airport.

____10. It is always happened right after a rain storm.

EDITING FOCUS

In English, many verbs can be used in the active or passive voice. You must decide between the active or passive voice. Compare these sentences:

(A) The teacher **returned** the exams on Monday.

(B) The exams **were returned** on Monday.

The two sentences have basically the same meaning, but the emphasis changes according to which subject the writer uses. In sentence A, the writer focuses on the teacher, while in sentence B the focus is on the exams.

FORMING THE PASSIVE VOICE

1. The passive voice is formed with the verb *be* + past participle. The tense is shown by the form of *be*. The verb *be* must agree with the subject.

Present		
Simple present	*am / is / are* + past participle	The newsletter **is distributed** worldwide.
Present progressive	*am / is / are + being* + past participle	A new library **is being built.**
Present perfect	*has / have + been* + past participle	The house **has** just **been painted.**

Past		
Simple past	*was / were* + past participle	The books **were returned** on time.
Past progressive	*was / were + being* + past participle	When I got to the plane, the doors **were being closed.**
Past perfect	*had + been* + past participle	The dinner **had been prepared** before we arrived.

Future		
Simple future	*will be* + past participle	We **will be tested** on this material.
Be going to	*am / is / are going to + be* + past participle	The show **is going to be held** next month.
Future perfect	*will have been* + past participle	We **will have been given** the information to register by then.

NOTE: The progressive forms of the present perfect, past perfect, future, and future perfect are very rarely used in the passive voice.

2. Modals using the passive voice can be formed in the present/future and the past.

Modals		
Present/future modals	modal + *be* + past participle	The computer can be upgraded.
Past time modals	modal + *have been* + past participle	The traffic delays must have been caused by the snow.

3. Infinitives and gerunds may be used in the passive voice.

Infinitives and Gerunds		
Verbs + Infinitives	verb + *to be* + past participle	The children like to be kissed before they go to bed.
Verbs + Gerunds	verb + *being* + past participle	He dislikes being treated like a child.

NOTE: In passive sentences with adverbs of time or frequency, the adverb usually follows *be, have,* or the modal auxiliary.

> The building is *still* being renovated.
> The parade has *always* been held on Thanksgiving.
> This door should *never* be locked.

USING THE PASSIVE VOICE

1. Use the passive voice in the following circumstances:
- when the person or thing doing the action (the agent) is obvious, unknown, or unimportant.

> **Many trees were planted to replace those lost in the fire.**
> *(The focus is on why the trees were planted. Who planted the trees is unknown or unimportant.)*

> **The house was built in 1860.**
> *(The focus is on when the house was built, not on who built it.)*

> **Tobacco is grown in the South.**
> *(The focus is on where tobacco is grown, not by whom.)*

- when you don't want to mention the person doing the action.

> **Several failing grades were received at the end of the class.**

> **The information was secretly given to the reporter before it was released to the public.**

> **The new law was passed without our knowledge.**

- when you want to emphasize the receiver of the action or the result of the action.

> **International students are sometimes housed in the homes of local families when they come to study for short periods of time.**

> **A new telephone system that should increase our sales volume is being installed.**

> **Children can be taught good manners when they are very young.**

- when you are describing a process.

> **After the specimens were collected and placed on the slides, the slides were observed under the microscope.**

> **The eggs are beaten until they are creamy, and then the sugar and butter are added.**

> **The wheel is attached to the axle before the nuts are tightened and the hubcap is attached.**

NOTE: The doer of the action may or may not be mentioned. If the writer knows who performs an action, usually the active voice is used. However, sometimes even when the writer knows who performs the action, he or she will use the passive with the *by*-phrase in order to focus on the subject. In the following sentence, the focus is on the two papers.

> **This paper was written *by an undergraduate student*, but that paper was written *by a graduate student*.**

2. Only transitive verbs (verbs that can take a direct object) may be used in the passive voice. Intransitive verbs (verbs that cannot have a direct object) cannot be made passive. The following is a list of some commonly used intransitive verbs.

appear	belong	exist	seem
arrive	come	happen	sleep
be	die	occur	rise

The car accident **happened** at the corner of Sixth Avenue and Main Street.

NOT

The car accident was happened at the corner of Sixth Avenue and Main Street.

> **TIP**
>
> Use a dictionary to check if a verb is transitive or intransitive before forming it in the passive voice. At the same time, check that the past participle form that you are using is correct.

3. Sentences often contain past participle adjectives that look like passive verbs. In these sentences, however, no action is taking place. The adjectives describe an existing situation or state.

Kendall is **concerned** about her grade in the class.

Dat and Amir are **worried** that they may miss their plane flight.

We are **involved** in the International Students Organization.

> **TIP**
>
> In spoken English, it is common to use the verb *get* to form the passive voice; however, this is considered informal, and it is generally better in written English to use the verb *be*. Edit for the overuse of the verb *get* in your writing.
>
> | **Preferred** | His first research project **was** published last week. |
> |---|---|
> | **Informal** | His first research project **got** published last week. |

SELF CHECK

Correct the errors in the passive voice.

1. I was transfer to the highest group in our math class.

2. Bacterial infections were existed before the Paleozoic Era.

3. Many new books are writing each year.

4. The award will be gave at the ceremony tonight.

5. I hope to accept at this university.

EDITING PRACTICE

1 *Put a check (✓) next to the sentences that use the passive or active voice correctly. Correct the sentences that have errors.*

____ 1. We think that the research will be finished next year.

____ 2. Always a meal is served after the lecture.

____ 3. Children need to be taking care of by their parents.

____ 4. She is belonging to the academic fraternity on campus.

____ 5. The fire was put out very quickly.

____ 6. Most crimes are commit in urban areas.

____ 7. It is assumed that the senator will resign soon.

____ 8. At my birthday party, the candles were blew out by my little brother.

____ 9. The number of graduates has been risen each year.

____ 10. Cancer is caused by environmental factors often.

____ 11. We denied being given the exam before the test day.

____ 12. Security measures must develop to prevent another occurrence of spying.

2 *In the following paragraph, the underlined verbs are not correct. Write the correct verb form above each underlined verb.*

The Olympic Games (1) <u>are believe</u> to be one of the most important sporting events. They (2) <u>are seeing</u> as athletically, economically, politically, and socially significant for the host city as well. The Games (3) <u>are seeked</u> by countless nations so that the host city and country (4) <u>can present</u> to the world in a positive light. Cities such as Sydney, Barcelona, Nagano, and Lillehammer (5) <u>still remembered</u> for the wonderful shows they put on for the world during the two weeks the Olympic Games (6) <u>held</u> in those cities. On the other hand, cities that do a poor job of hosting the Olympics (7) <u>are not allow</u> to forget it. Some Olympic Games (8) <u>will be remember</u> for tragic events that (9) <u>were happened</u> there, such as the Munich Games in 1972 and the Atlanta Games in 1996. For the most part, however, the Games have been a time of peace, friendship, and enthusiasm for all involved, athletes and spectators alike. It is hoped that this wonderful tradition will continue well into the future and the tragedies (10) <u>are understood and not forget</u>.

3 *Read the following paragraph. Complete the paragraph with the active or passive form of each verb given. Use the time markers to help you choose the best verb tense.*

I believe that it is important to remember significant events by placing landmarks, memorials, or statues where these events _____. After WWI and WWII, many
1. occur

statues _____ in capitals around the world so that we would not forget the wars
2. build

and the people who took part in them. Places of natural beauty are also important to mark in

some way. National Parks _____ in the United States for the first time in 1912.
3. create

Since that point in time, many more scenic places around the world _____ as
4. designate

permanent spots of natural beauty. This means that in the future these areas

_____ and will remain in their natural state.
5. cannot, develop

I think it is also important to remember events that don't have worldwide significance but

hold community importance. These should also _____. Specifically, I am thinking
6. remember

about an event that _____ in my hometown in Taiwan five years ago. A school bus
7. happen

full of young children was traveling on a rural road on the way to school when it

_____ from behind by a large truck. Sadly, several children who were sitting in the
8. hit

rear of the bus _____, and many more _____ in this horrible
9. kill   **10. injure**

accident. Even though the tragedy _____ to be an accident, I believe the
11. seem

community needs to do something to remember the innocent victims. Perhaps a tree or a garden

could _____ as a living memorial to these small children. I believe that this is an
12. plant

important way for people to remember significant events and to heal the sadness.

4 *The following paragraph has ten errors in the use of the passive voice. Find and correct the errors.*

Watching television still seems to be the preferred leisure activity of many students. Even

in the age of the Internet, video games, and various interactive media, students consistently

mention television as the way they like to relax. After conducting my informal survey, I was both

surprised and pleased by the results. I thought that the Internet would be give as the most popular

free-time activity; however, I was wrong. Television listed as the most popular leisure activity.

Although much of the programming on TV is of low quality, the television shows that students watch are generally of high quality. Soap operas and "trash" TV were appeared on some students' lists of favorite shows, but the majority listed educational programs. Some differences found between male and female TV viewers. The shows that are watch by males tend to be sports competitions and scientific programming. The programs that are preferring by females are the interview shows and historical documentaries. Both male and female students agreed that political and news shows do not hold their interest. I thought nationality might make a difference in viewing preferences, but program preferences not affected by this. Even though those surveyed are belonged to different sex, age, and nationality groups, television viewing habits were find to be almost universal. It is important to note, however, that this survey included only university students, and this may have been affected the results.

WRITING TOPICS

Choose one of the topics below, and write at least one paragraph. Be sure to use the passive voice. After you complete your first draft, concentrate on editing your work. Keep in mind the editing practice from this chapter.

1. Pick a process such as telling a good story, making a cake, or fixing a car and explain how to do it well. What steps should be followed? How much time is needed to complete the process? Where is the process done? Be sure to tell what you like about this process.

2. Select a recent or historical event from any place around the world. Explain the significance this event has for you and for other people. Where did the event occur? How was the world affected by this event? How was this event viewed by the people closest to it and by others around the world?

Go to pages 102 and 104 for more practice with the passive voice.

CHAPTER 5

Coordination and Parallel Structure

PRETEST

Check your understanding of coordination and parallel structure. Put a check (✓) next to the sentences that are correct.

_____ 1. The passage discusses the American value of independence, it also points out other common values.

_____ 2. The results of racism can never be anything except negative, unfairness, and unjust.

_____ 3. The business world provides financial rewards, and people tend to pursue these rather than the emotional rewards that friends and family provide.

_____ 4. Simon loves English literature, but he wants to take three English classes next semester.

_____ 5. Not only smoking damages your lungs, but it also decreases bone density.

_____ 6. People make promises, yet they do not always keep them.

EDITING FOCUS

By using coordination, a writer gives equal importance to two or more ideas. Coordinating conjunctions join two or more similar grammatical parts such as words, phrases, or clauses. Different coordinating conjunctions show the relationship between the parts.

In the following example, notice how the conjunction *but* joins two independent clauses and at the same time shows the contrast between them.

Engineers use math extensively, but they need good language skills, too.

As a writer and editor, you must select the appropriate coordinating conjunction for the meaning you wish to convey, and make sure it is in the right place in the sentence.

FORMING SENTENCES WITH COORDINATING AND CORRELATIVE CONJUNCTIONS

1. Coordinating conjunctions include:

   and, but, so, or, nor, yet, for

   Correlative, or paired conjunctions, include:

   both . . . and, not only…but also, either . . . or, neither . . . nor

2. Coordinating and correlative conjunctions join:
   - words

     Masis and Yuri fled the war in Armenia.

     The book was neither well-written nor interesting.

   - phrases

     They are glad to be out of their country but are still proud of their homeland.

     Both the students who won the awards and the teachers who taught them were there.

   - dependent clauses

     If you are good and if we have enough time, we will stop and get ice cream.

   - independent clauses

     They had to leave their country, for they had no future there.

     Yesterday it not only rained, but it also snowed.

3. When two independent clauses are joined with a coordinating or correlative conjunction, a comma goes before the conjunction. No comma is needed when two phrases or words are joined.

   Comma   **Students can develop these skills in classes, or the skills can be learned through on-the-job training.**

   Not only is James an excellent teacher, but he is also a talented guitar player.

No comma	Computer scientists **and** engineers need strong problem-solving skills.
	Both lunch **and** dinner will be served at the conference.
	Strong problem-solving skills are important **but** are not the only necessary skills.
	Neither the campus bookstore **nor** the one downtown has the book I need.

TIP

Coordinating conjunctions show the relationship between two or more sentence parts, so these conjunctions generally appear between sentence parts rather than at the beginning of a sentence. Avoid beginning a sentence with a coordinating conjunction.

Preferred	Election volunteers can mail campaign literature, **or** they can telephone registered voters.
Less formal	Election volunteers can mail campaign literature. **Or** they can telephone registered voters.
Preferred	We arrived at the sale late, **so** we missed the best deals.
Less formal	We arrived at the sale late. **So** we missed the best deals.

4. In sentences with correlative conjunctions, the subject that is closer to the verb determines if the verb is singular or plural.

> **Not only** my best friend, **but** *my parents are* also here.

> **Not only** my parents, **but** *my best friend is* also here.

5. Use coordinating conjunctions as one way to avoid run-on sentences and comma splice errors.

Run-on	The unemployment rate decreased last month 200,000 jobs were added in the workplace.
Comma splice	The unemployment rate decreased last month, 200,000 jobs were added in the workplace.
Correct sentence	The unemployment rate decreased last month, **and** 200,000 jobs were added in the workplace.

6. Coordinating conjunctions cannot be combined with other conjunctions within the same sentence.

Incorrect	**Although** the union signed a new contract, **but** not all of the members are happy.
Correct	The union signed a new contract, **but** not all of the members are happy.

USING COORDINATING AND CORRELATIVE CONJUNCTIONS

1. Each coordinating conjunction has a different use.

Coordinating Conjunction	Use	Example
and	to add information	Daniela is going downtown to meet a friend **and** to hear a lecture.
but	to show contrast	The downtown area will be crowded, **but** Daniela really wants to hear the lecture.
or	to give a choice	Daniela hasn't decided if she is going to drive herself **or** take the bus.
yet	to show contrast	Daniela sees her friend frequently, **yet** she still looks forward to their conversations.
so	to show a result	Max is a foreign language major, **so** he will take French and Italian classes this year.
for	to show a reason	Juan is taking classes in four different departments, **for** he has not decided on his major yet.

NOTE: The conjunction *for* means *because*, but *it* is not used very often to express this meaning. The preferred connector is *because*.

2. Use paired or correlative conjunctions rather than coordinating conjunctions to add emphasis to the parts being joined or to express a choice.

To add emphasis use *both . . . and* or *not only . . . but also.*

> **Both** solar **and** wind energy are alternatives to oil and coal.

> Computer hackers **not only** slow business **but also** damage computer systems.

To emphasize that both are negative use *neither . . . nor.*

> **Neither** men **nor** women prefer newspapers to television news.

To express a choice use *either . . . or.*

> He wants a computer made by **either** Dell **or** Compaq.

> **TIP**
>
> Since *that* is not a coordinating conjunction, it cannot be used in the same way as *and, but, so, or, nor, yet,* or *for.*
>
> The council meeting will be televised, **so** all citizens can watch the debate.
>
> The council meeting will be televised, **and** all citizens can watch the debate
>
> NOT
> The council meeting will be televised, ***that*** all citizens can watch the debate.

SELF CHECK 1

Correct the errors in coordination.

1. We worked all night, so we didn't meet our deadline.

2. I finished the coffee, it was bitter.

3. My study group worked hard, that we finished the project early.

4. The lake was closed due to contamination but people were still walking along the shoreline.

5. Neither my sister nor my parents is here.

PARALLEL STRUCTURE

1. When you join words, phrases, or clauses with coordinating conjunctions, they must be parallel. That is, they must be the same grammatical structure.

    > **Russian cosmonauts, American astronauts, *and* private citizens** are now traveling to the International Space Station. *(nouns)*

    > They **are finishing** their experiments ***and* (are) leaving** for home soon. *(verbs)*

    > Their experiments in space are **expensive *but* important** for advancing our knowledge. *(adjectives)*

    > The astronauts try **to exercise *or* to work out** on a treadmill every day while they are in space. *(infinitives)*

    > **Working, eating, *and* sleeping** side by side in such a small space requires cooperation. *(gerunds)*

    > The results of their experiments will be used **in many industries, in a variety of ways, *and* for years to come.** *(prepositional phrases)*

    > **Astronauts train for possible emergencies at the Space Station, *but* fortunately, they have never had to use this training.** *(clauses)*

    NOTE: When you write more than two parallel items, use commas to separate them. The comma before the conjunction is optional but often preferred in academic and literary writing.

    > It is difficult to **work, study, *and* take care** of small children at the same time.

2. When words, phrases, or clauses are joined with the paired conjunctions *not only . . . but also, both . . . and, either . . . or,* or *neither . . . nor,* they must be parallel in form.

    >   noun   noun
    > ***Not only* ranchers *but also* farmers** are affected economically by government policies.

    >   noun   noun
    > ***Both* Jenny *and* Judy** play water polo.

verb phrase   verb phrase

We will *either* see a movie *or* go out to dinner tonight.

adjective   adjective

My son was *neither* anxious *nor* upset at the doctor's office.

3. When using the paired conjunction *not only . . . but also* to connect independent clauses, the word order is inverted if the sentence begins with *not only*. For verbs other than *be*, you must add an auxiliary verb after *not only*.

Regular word order   Debbie *not only* likes to swim, *but* she *also* likes to run.

Inverted word order   *Not only* does Debbie like to swim, *but* she *also* likes to run.

Regular word order   There is *not only* an apricot tree in the yard, *but* there is *also* a plum tree.

Inverted word order   *Not only* is there an apricot tree in the yard, *but* there is *also* a plum tree.

SELF CHECK 2

Correct the errors in parallel structure.

1. Vicki has improved her writing by learning grammar rules, and she edits carefully.

2. Ms. Lee is searching for a new job and moves to a new house at the same time.

3. My best friend is good at listening, thinking deeply about a problem, and he always gives good advice.

4. My roommate was neither anxious nor relaxing the night before her exams.

5. I will either study painting or sculpture.

EDITING PRACTICE

1 *Put a check (✓) next to the sentences that use coordination and parallel structure correctly. Correct the sentences that have errors.*

____ 1. Both tea and coffee are popular beverages throughout the world.

____ 2. Neither the play is entertaining nor funny.

____ 3. Unaffordable medical care keeps people away from the doctor they become sicker and medical costs increase.

____ 4. My grandmother taught me lessons such as being generous with others and being satisfied with what I have.

____ 5. Mr. Bustillo was very well prepared for the speech, so he didn't do a very good job.

_____ 6. Civil rights groups are not afraid to stand up for their beliefs and to challenge those who might disagree with them.

_____ 7. The current generation of students cannot imagine working in a traditional nine to five job and having only two weeks of vacation each year.

_____ 8. Sissela loves science. So she is going to major in biology.

_____ 9. Children learn a lot from storytelling important life lessons are taught in an entertaining manner.

_____ 10. The antique photograph illustrates the struggle, sacrifice, and hardship that past generations experienced.

_____ 11. When I received my diploma, my parents looked at me and smile.

_____ 12. Next winter Nasim wants an unforgettable vacation like helicopter skiing in Canada. Or snow camping on a glacier in New Zealand.

2 *Read the following paragraph. Complete the paragraph with the correct coordinating conjunction.*

Over the last decade _____ two, the development of self-esteem has become a
                              1. or / and

popular topic. It has even become an industry with thousands of books, websites, seminars,

_____ dollars devoted to the building of self-esteem. Some of these sources tell people to
2. or / and

visualize success, to recite affirmations, _____ to heal wounds from the past. Conventional
                                            3. and / but

wisdom teaches that in order to be successful we cannot have too much self-doubt. In other

words, we must develop a sense of our own worth before we can experience success. This may

sound logical, _____ some people question this approach to the development of self-
               4. but / and

esteem. They wonder which comes first, self-esteem _____ success. Another point of view
                                                    5. and / or

is that people must first experience success before they can develop self-esteem, _____
                                                                                  6. yet / for

they will not be able to feel good about themselves without feeling successful. It's difficult to feel

positive about ourselves before we achieve success, _____ it is necessary to take risks in
                                                     7. so / or

order to gain self-worth. The anxiety we feel due to self-doubt can be positive if used in the

correct way. If someone has a fear of flying, public speaking, _____ taking a new job, he or
                                                              8. yet / or

she should do it in order to get over the fear and to build self-esteem. It is also necessary to have

goals, _____ when feelings of doubt begin to get in the way, the direction _____
       9. so / but   **10. for / or**

goal is still clear. Regardless of the approach one takes to gain it, most agree that self-esteem is

necessary for a productive and successful life.

3 *In the following essay, the underlined sentences have errors in coordinating conjunctions or parallel structure. Write your corrections above each underlined sentence.*

Power is the control or influence that individuals or groups hold over each other. This influence can be exerted in various ways. The authority a parent holds over a child, the physical force one person has over another, the influence large countries have over smaller ones, and the will our minds have over our bodies are all examples of power. (1) <u>Power is even evident when love is involved individuals behave against their will simply to please their loved ones</u>. In addition, by making one group feel inferior, another group may be able to exert its power. (2) <u>Power is an interesting phenomenon that doesn't always have to be used in a negative way, it is an influence that people should use wisely</u>.

An interesting thing happened to me when I was a senior in high school. (3) <u>I knew my parents had authority over me I didn't fully realize the influence of their love until it was time to select a college</u>. (4) <u>I had been working hard for four years in order to be accepted at a particular college, yet I was thrilled when my acceptance letter arrived</u>. When my parents realized that I would really be moving and living hundreds of miles from home, they strongly encouraged me to select another university closer to our city. (5) <u>Although I had worked, dream, and hope to attend my first choice university, I almost gave up that dream for my parents</u>. (6) <u>Their love was a strong influence over me. But I knew what I wanted</u>. (7) <u>Not only I was strong enough to stand up against their power, but I was also able to rationally explain my decision</u>. Both my parents and I now know I made the right decision by leaving home, but it has been difficult for my parents to see their influence decreasing in my life. (8) <u>The various forms of power are interesting to observe and learning from</u>. There is nothing worse than to see any form of power used in an unproductive way.

The following paragraph has ten errors in the formal use of coordination and parallel structure. Find and correct the errors.

People need to have their own personal space. Even though humans are social animals, they need a place where they can get away from others, feel safe, and to be in charge. This personal space may be a neighborhood, a home, or a room. Or even half of a room! Our space is apparent to others because we personalize it. One of the reasons we feel secure in our space is because our personal possessions surround us. Studies show that people with more belongings around them feel more attached to a particular spot, and this is especially obvious in dormitories where personal space is at a minimum. Both possessions mark where a person's territory ends and the next person's begins. Students bring personal items such as computers, pictures, stereos, and stuffed animals from home their new space will feel familiar to them. I have done this, too. I define my personal space but help others know who I am by putting up posters of Michael Jordan. When people come into my room, they will see my love of basketball, that I admire Michael Jordan. Not only I brought my basketball posters, but I also have basketballs, basketball shoes, basketball jerseys, basketball magazines, and everything else related to basketball on my half of the dorm room. I brought all these belongings from home, yet now I feel half of the dorm room is my own. This has helped me feel secure during my first months in a new environment. My roommate has personalized his side of the room by hooking up all his electronic equipment. His stereo, CDs, VCR, DVD player, and TV define his strong interest in technology. If we drive down any street or walk into any home, we can easily see the variety of ways in which people personalize their space but this human need is even more obvious in the confined space of a dormitory room. We all like to believe we are unique but we all share a universal trait that is surprisingly strong—all humans need a space that they can call their own.

WRITING TOPICS

Choose one of the topics below, and write at least one paragraph. Be sure to use several different coordinating conjunctions and parallel structure. After you complete your first draft, concentrate on editing your work. Keep in mind the editing practice from this chapter.

1. Many people prefer to read fiction while others read only nonfiction. Which do you prefer to read? Explain why you like one type of writing over others, and give examples of stories, novels, or articles that you have enjoyed.

2. Carefully describe an advertisement that you have recently seen or heard. The advertisement could be from television, radio, magazines, billboards, or any number of other sources. Explain why this advertisement caught your eye and why you think it is particularly effective or ineffective.

Go to pages 102 and 105 for more practice with coordination and parallel structure.

CHAPTER 6

Adjective Clauses

PRE**TEST**

Check your understanding of adjective clauses. Put a check (✓) next to the sentences that are correct.

_____ 1.   The company that I want to work for is small.

_____ 2.   The book is overdue that I borrowed from the library.

_____ 3.   Countries whose gun laws are strict have few gun deaths.

_____ 4.   Alan's father, which has a Ph.D. in chemical engineering, has high expectations for his son.

_____ 5.   The hero, who is in every scene of the first half of the movie, unexpectedly disappears in the second half.

_____ 6.   My friends recommended the restaurant that is on the corner of Irvine Avenue and Seventeenth Street.

_____ 7.   Countries, that have earthquakes, need strict building codes.

_____ 8.   Dr. Kaufman who teaches physiology will retire soon.

_____ 9.   The concert tickets which Carol and I bought are in my purse.

_____10.   The winter Jan worked at the ski resort was the best of her life.

EDITING FOCUS

Adjective clauses, also called relative clauses, are like adjectives because they identify or give more information about nouns or pronouns. Use adjective clauses to combine sentences and to make your writing more descriptive and interesting. As a writer, you must decide when adjective clauses can improve your writing and know how to construct these clauses. Compare these two examples:

- We love the old house. It has a huge pear tree.

- We love the old house **that has a huge pear tree**.

Both examples convey the same meaning, but the second example uses an adjective clause and expresses the same information in a more concise and sophisticated way.

FORMING ADJECTIVE CLAUSES

1. An adjective clause is a dependent clause so it cannot stand alone. It must be connected to an independent clause to form a complex sentence. An adjective clause is introduced by a relative pronoun such as *that, who, whom, which,* and *whose.* The noun or pronoun that the relative pronoun refers to is called the antecedent.

2. In most cases, the adjective clause directly follows the noun it is identifying or describing (the antecedent).

   The surprise birthday *party* **that Grant and Bob gave for Stella** was a lot of fun.

   NOT
   The surprise birthday party was a lot of fun that Grant and Bob gave for Stella.

   The man **who(m) we spoke to** gave us good advice.

   NOT
   The man gave us good advice whom we spoke to.

3. Do not use double pronouns within the adjective clause.

   Joanna's father is *the kind of person* **who never gets mad**.

   NOT
   Joanna's father is the kind of person who he never gets mad.

   This is the *program* **that Samuel and I wrote for our computer science class**.

   NOT
   This is the program that Samuel and I wrote it for our computer science class.

4. When a relative pronoun is the subject of the adjective clause, use a subject pronoun.

- *who* or *that* for people

> Susanna baby-sits for her neighbor. Her neighbor has five children.

> Susanna baby-sits for her *neighbor* **who** has five children.

> The girls live next door. The girls are really nice.

> The *girls* **that** live next door are really nice.

- *which* or *that* for things

> John wrote a research paper. The research paper analyzes the causes of depression.

> John wrote a *research paper* **that** analyzes the causes of depression.

> I submitted the two projects. The two projects were due today.

> I submitted the two *projects,* **which** were due today.

5. When the relative pronoun is the object of the adjective clause, use an object pronoun.

- *whom, who,* or *that* for people

> Harry Truman governed during the late 1940s. My grandmother knew Harry Truman.

> *Harry Truman,* **who(m)** my grandmother knew, governed during the late 1940s.

- *which* or *that* for things

> I bought a computer yesterday. The computer I bought will be delivered to the store tomorrow.

> The *computer* **that** I bought yesterday will be delivered to the store tomorrow.

The relative pronoun can also be the object of a preposition.

> The car **that** Rose left her purse **in** was stolen.

> The car **in which** Rose left her purse was stolen. *(formal, academic English)*

> **NOTE:** When the relative pronoun is the object of the verb or object of a preposition, it can be omitted.
>
> > The computer **that** I ***bought*** yesterday will be delivered tomorrow.
> >
> > The computer I bought yesterday will be delivered tomorrow.
> >
> > The car **that** Rose left her purse ***in*** was stolen.
> >
> > The car Rose left her purse in was stolen.

6. When a relative pronoun replaces a possessive word, use *whose* + noun.

> *My sister's son* just went away to college. My sister feels lonely.

> My sister, **whose son** just went away to college, feels lonely.

> *The company's headquarters* are in Boston. The company has offices overseas.

> The company, **whose headquarters** are in Boston, has offices overseas.

In spoken English, *whose* and *who's* sound similar. In writing, be sure to use the contraction *who's* for *who is* and *who has* and the relative pronoun *whose* to show possession.

Who's going to the assembly?

Russell found the child *who's* been missing for a week.

I want to work for a company **whose** profits are growing.

7. Sentences with adjective clauses must follow all subject-verb agreement rules.
- The subject and verb of the independent clause must agree even if they are separated by an adjective clause.

    The chemistry **classes** *that I took last semester* **were** very interesting.

    NOT
    The chemistry classes that I took last semester was very interesting.

- The verb following the relative pronoun always has the same number as the antecedent.

    Our neighbors have a *dog* **that barks** all day long. *(singular)*

    The *boys* in my dorm **who play** water polo travel a lot with the team. *(plural)*

- The subject and verb within the relative clause must agree.

                 S V
    The *textbooks* **that she is buying** cost $250.

    NOT
    The textbooks that she are buying cost $250.

Mark the subjects and verbs in sentences that use adjective clauses. Put the letter *S* above subjects, the letter *V* above verbs, and make sure each pair agrees.

8. Restrictive adjective clauses (also called identifying or defining) do not require commas. A restrictive adjective clause supplies necessary information to identify the noun that it modifies. Restrictive adjective clauses are used more frequently than nonrestrictive adjective clauses.

    A *person* **who sells stocks and bonds** is called a stockbroker.
    (*The information in the adjective clause is necessary in order to know which person is being described.*)

    Do you know the *man* **who is at the table in the corner**?
    (*The information in the adjective clause is necessary in order to know which man is being referred to.*)

9. Nonrestrictive adjective clauses (also called nonidentifying or nondefining) require commas. A nonrestrictive clause supplies additional information, not necessary to identify the noun it modifies.

> We just read _One Hundred Years of Solitude_, **which is by Gabriel Garcia Marquez.**
> (_The additional information in the adjective clause is not necessary to identify the book._)

> _Ten Downing Street_, **where the prime minister of England lives,** is a plain-looking house.
> (_The additional information in the adjective clause is not necessary to identify the address._)

NOTE: Do not use the relative pronoun _that_ in a nonrestrictive adjective clause.

> Old Faithful, **which** is located in Yellowstone National Park, regularly shoots water and steam into the air.

> NOT
> Old Faithful, that is located in Yellowstone National Park, regularly shoots water and steam into the air.

10. Commas around an adjective clause can change the meaning of a sentence. Compare the meanings of the following sentences:

> The students, **who wanted to study French,** had to wait in line to register.
> (_The use of commas means that all of the students wanted to study French, and all of them had to wait in line._)

> The students **who wanted to study French** had to wait in line to register. The students who wanted to study German didn't have to wait in line.
> (_The lack of commas means that only some of the students wanted to study French. The adjective clause identifies which students had to wait in line._)

NOTE: Adjective clauses can be used to describe indefinite pronouns such as _someone, anyone, everything,_ and _other._

> _Someone_ **who wanted to speak with you** called but didn't leave a message.

> I don't know _anyone_ **who has a truck.**

USING ADJECTIVE CLAUSES

1. Use adjective clauses to combine ideas and make your sentences less short and repetitive.

> My friend is a medical student. She hopes to specialize in pediatrics.

> My friend, **who is a medical student,** hopes to specialize in pediatrics.

2. Use adjective clauses to make general sentences more specific or descriptive.

> **General**   They just finished a research project.

> **Descriptive**   They just finished a research project **that analyzes the effectiveness of grammar instruction in reading classes.**

3. The relative adverbs _where_ and _when_ can be used to introduce adjective clauses of place and time.

> We went to _Yellowstone_, **where** we saw Old Faithful.

> The _week_ **when** she was in the hospital was hard on her parents.

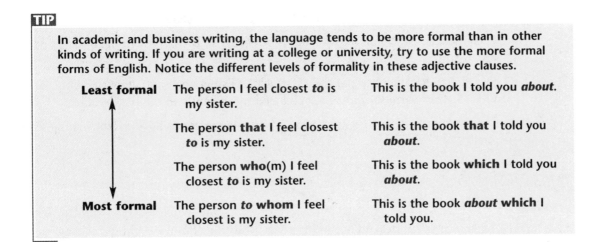

TIP

In academic and business writing, the language tends to be more formal than in other kinds of writing. If you are writing at a college or university, try to use the more formal forms of English. Notice the different levels of formality in these adjective clauses.

Least formal	The person I feel closest *to* is my sister.	This is the book I told you *about*.
	The person **that** I feel closest *to* is my sister.	This is the book **that** I told you *about*.
	The person **who**(m) I feel closest *to* is my sister.	This is the book **which** I told you *about*.
Most formal	The person *to whom* I feel closest is my sister.	This is the book *about* **which** I told you.

SELF CHECK

Correct the errors in adjective clauses.

1. Professor Simms, that we had for economics, is very fair.

2. Samuel Clemens who wrote *The Adventures of Huckleberry Finn* used the pen name Mark Twain.

3. The classes Sam is taking begins next week.

4. The interview with the director of operations went very well that I had yesterday.

5. His cousins went to a wedding ceremony that it was on the beach at sunset.

EDITING PRACTICE

1 *Put a check (✓) next to the sentences that use adjective clauses correctly. Correct the sentences that have errors.*

____ 1. Thoa's father, that used to play college football, is coaching the high school team.

____ 2. The blending of cultures that we see in the United States today has both good and bad points.

____ 3. The bulbs should bloom in the spring that we planted last winter.

____ 4. The ABC software company whose president just resigned is in financial trouble.

____ 5. St. John, which is a Caribbean island, is a tropical paradise.

____ 6. The 1992 demonstration is an example of the unrest that we are going to study it in sociology.

____ 7. Extremely competitive people who always want to win damages valuable friendships.

____ 8. The woman whom the story is about lives in a small New England town.

_____ 9. Galileo Galilei, whom never left Italy, was nonetheless known around the world.

_____ 10. The Tasman Sea, where the poisonous box jellyfish lives, is the home of other deadly sea creatures.

_____ 11. The Puerto Rican culture of the 1950s which Esmeralda Santiago writes about in *When I Was Puerto Rican* has not changed significantly in the last decades.

_____ 12. Professor Williams, whose class is on Wednesday nights, is an excellent writing teacher.

2 *Read the following paragraph. Complete the paragraph with the correct relative pronoun, relative adverb, or neither (Ø).*

D.H. Lawrence celebrates old age in his poem *Beautiful Old Age*. Although old age is a

stage of life _____ is not always valued, Lawrence puts into words some of its positive

1. when / that

points. He says that a person _____ has led a truthful life will live happily into old age.

2. who / which

Old age should be a time _____ people feel peace from having lived a full life. Wrinkled

3. when / where

skin, _____ is inevitable, is a sign of wisdom and not of deterioration. If people believe

4. that / which

Lawrence's words, then maturity ought to be a stage _____ we look forward to, and the

5. who / that

elderly person _____ we fear becoming ought to be looked at as someone _____

6. Ø / which   **7. Ø / where**

we strive to be. Two people _____ fit this description of beautiful old age are my great

8. whom / who

grandmother and my great-aunt. Both women have lived honest lives _____ have been

9. when / that

filled with hard work and family. They are being rewarded for their work as children,

grandchildren, and great grandchildren honor them daily. This is the old age that I hope to have

one day—the old age that D.H. Lawrence describes and the old age _____ my great

10. when / that

grandmother and great-aunt are living.

3 *In the following paragraph, five of the underlined adjective clauses are not correct. Find the errors and write the corrections above each clause.*

There are many examples today of the cultural influences (1) <u>that powerful countries have

on less powerful countries</u>. English influence in Antigua, French influence in Vietnam, and

American influence in Puerto Rico are all examples of less dominant cultures absorbing the styles

and traditions of more dominant cultures. According to Jamacia Kincaid, an Antiguan writer, the

gardens (2) <u>that naturally grow in Antigua</u> have no order to them; they are wild and natural.

However, the British influence, (3) <u>that emphasizes order and organization</u>, can be seen in some of the gardening styles of wealthy Antiguans. Christmas trees (4) <u>which originated in Germany</u> have also found their way to Antigua due to British influence. In Vietnam, the French influence, (5) <u>which was even more apparent years ago</u>, is still obvious today. Vietnamese food and architecture, (6) <u>which are considered traditional</u>, have a French touch. The French language, (7) <u>which was once the language of the educated and influential in Vietnam</u>, still holds a position of importance. In Puerto Rico, language also plays an influential role. Spanish, (8) <u>that is the primary language in Puerto Rico</u>, has been replaced by English in some schools and institutions. In addition to the English language, American food and music are now part of the Puerto Rican way of life. Many Puerto Ricans can still remember the day several decades ago (9) <u>when Americans came to their small towns to "educate" them about diet and hygiene</u>. Many (10) <u>whom accepted this at the time</u> learned to resent it later. In this day and age, it is hard to stop or even to ignore worldwide influences. Cultural influence is a phenomenon (11) <u>who's importance shouldn't go unnoticed</u>.

 4 *The following paragraph has ten errors in the use of adjective clauses. Find and correct the errors.*

The object that I am looking at is a three-dimensional rectangle, although sometimes this object can be the shape of a cube or a sphere. Five sides are made of glass, that is clear, and there is either a removable top or no top at all. One usually finds this object inside a house or office in a room when people are likely to meet, such as the living room, family room, or kitchen. This object is not mobile. It often has a small motor that keep the environment inside the rectangle clean. Even with this motor, the object has to be cleaned every few weeks. Plants may also be found inside of it that help keep this object clean. Next to the plants, there are sometimes figurines that they are set in brightly colored rocks. Both adults and children like this object. Some people who they have stressful lives find this object soothing and peaceful to look at. People whom have these objects usually love animals. Animals use this object for a home that live in fresh and salt water. The animals, that live in this object, make good pets for a person who he is allergic to cats and dogs. Do you know what this object is?

WRITING TOPICS

Choose one of the topics below, and write at least one paragraph. Be sure to use adjective clauses. After you complete your first draft, concentrate on editing your work. Keep in mind the editing practice from this chapter.

1. Pick an object that is in your sight right now, and describe it without giving the object's name. In addition to a thorough description of this object, include what this object is used for, where it is usually found, and who uses it.

2. How is the education that you are receiving now different from the education you received as a child or in another country? Discuss differences such as those you find in social life, academic pressure, testing, grading, and extracurricular activities.

Go to pages 104 and 106 for more practice with adjective clauses.

CHAPTER 7

Adverb Clauses

PRETEST

Check your understanding of adverb clauses. Put a check (✓) next to the sentences that are correct.

____ 1. Since I found a parking space close to my classroom, I still didn't make it to class on time.

____ 2. Even though it is difficult and expensive to travel to the Arctic Circle it is worth the effort.

____ 3. Although I studied for the quiz, but I still received a low grade.

____ 4. That actress is so well known that she has a hard time being in public places.

____ 5. While we were studying at Kylie's house last night.

____ 6. Mr. and Mrs. Skinner will choose to live wherever they can easily visit their grandchildren.

____ 7. We have enjoyed watching television since we got cable.

____ 8. He still doesn't feel comfortable in the ocean because he has been swimming for many years.

____ 9. After they were married, they moved to a new apartment.

EDITING FOCUS

Adverb clauses allow a writer to describe relationships such as contrast, time, and cause and effect. They help a writer to combine short sentences into longer, complex ones that show the relationship between the two. Compare examples (A) and (B). With the adverb clause, sentence B reads more smoothly and emphasizes the contrast found in the two original sentences.

> **(A) I finished the novel that you recommended. I didn't like it very much.**
>
> **(B) I finished the novel that you recommended, even though I didn't like it very much.**

FORMING COMPLEX SENTENCES WITH ADVERB CLAUSES

1. An adverb clause is a dependent clause that begins with a subordinating conjunction such as *because, after,* or *although.* An adverb clause must be connected to an independent, or main, clause. Read the complex sentences below and the rules for forming them that follow.

    independent clause   adverb clause

    I don't understand the concept *because* it is very complicated.

    subordinating
    conjunction

    adverb clause   independent clause

    ***After* it rained for a week**, there was a lot of pollution in the bay.

    subordinating
    conjunction

2. An adverb clause cannot stand alone. It must be attached to an independent clause or a fragment results.

Complete sentence	We lived in the city **before we moved to the mountains.**
Fragment	Before we moved to the mountains.
Complete sentence	**Although the weather forecast isn't good,** I think we should go.
Fragment	Although the weather forecast isn't good.

3. Use a comma after an adverb clause that begins a sentence.

    > **Although Armando is now working in the business world,** he hopes to move into education.

    Do not use a comma when the independent clause comes before the adverb clause.

    > **My daughter will never have a large salary because she wants to be a forest ranger.**

    NOTE: If the independent clause is followed by an adverb that shows contrast or concession (*although, though, even though, while,* or *whereas*), you can use a comma to separate the clauses.

    > **Armando is an excellent writing student, whereas Antonio is a very poor writing student.**

4. Subordinating conjunctions cannot be combined with other conjunctions within the same sentence.

Even though we didn't speak the language, we were able to communicate well.

NOT
Even though we didn't speak the language, **but** we were able to communicate well.

subordinating	coordinating
conjunction	conjunction

5. Do not use a prepositional phrase when you need a subordinating conjunction. A prepositional phrase cannot be used to connect two clauses.

Because the wind was blowing so hard, the tree in our front yard fell over.

subordinating
conjunction

NOT
Because of the wind was blowing so hard, the tree in our front yard fell over.

prepositional
phrase

6. Place the conjunction in the correct clause.

Because Jason's new suit was too tight, he didn't wear it to the wedding.

NOT
Jason's suit was too tight because he didn't wear it to the wedding.

USING ADVERB CLAUSES

1. Use adverb clauses to emphasize the relationship between ideas and to connect short sentences. Notice that a subordinating conjunction makes one idea less important than the other.

independent clause	independent clause
(equally important)	(equally important)

He washed his car for the first time in two months.　He has a date tonight.

independent clause	adverb clause
(more important)	(less important)

He washed his car for the first time in two months *because* he has a date tonight.

subordinating
conjunction

2. Subordinating conjunctions can be categorized according to their meaning.

Time	*after, as, as soon as, before, since, until, when, whenever, while*
	We decided not to leave the house **after** our guests had arrived.
	As soon as the plums are ripe, I am going to make jam.
Reason/cause	*as, due to the fact that, because, since*
	Since you love dogs, we bought you a puppy for your birthday.
	The old oak tree died **due to the fact that** it had root disease.
Concession	*although, despite the fact that, even though, in spite of the fact that, though*
	We loved the movie, **even though** all the reviews were bad.
	Although it may be below freezing, my children love to play outside.
Contrast	*whereas, while*
	We took the train and arrived in one hour, **whereas** Pete drove and arrived in thirty minutes.
	While Tom is a good math student and a poor English student, Pam does well in English and poorly in math.
Result	*so . . . that, such . . . that*
	I was **so** busy **that** I forgot to wish her a happy birthday. *(adjective)*
	Marta drives **so** quickly **that** I don't like to be a passenger in her car. *(adverb)*
	We had **such** a busy day **that** we were late for dinner. *(noun phrase)*
Purpose	*so that, in order that*
	Fatima wants to move closer to school **so that** she doesn't spend so much time commuting.
	In order that we don't have to pay a fine, we must get our taxes in on time.
Place	*where, wherever*
	I will move to **wherever** I get a job.
	There has to be a swimming pool **where** he can work out.

3. The conjunction you use must create a logical relationship between the ideas in the sentence.

Incorrect or illogical	Brandon sucked his thumb **because** he was three years old. *(Brandon's age is not the reason that he sucked his thumb. Many three-year-olds do not suck their thumbs.)*
Correct or logical	He sucked his thumb **because** he was tired.
Correct or logical	He sucked his thumb **until** he was three years old.
Incorrect or illogical	Most students have to study **while** they can pass their classes. *(Passing a class is usually the result of studying. While shows contrast or time, neither of which is a logical choice in this sentence.)*
Correct or logical	Most students have to study **so that** they can pass their classes.
Correct or logical	Most students have to study **while** they are in school.

4. Some conjunctions (i.e. *as, since, while*) have more than one meaning.

as	As Paul and I were leaving the house, the phone rang. *(time)*
	My older cousin received many scholarships **as** he was the best student in the school district. *(reason/cause)*
since	It has not rained **since** the last time I went camping. *(time)*
	Since you and I are neighbors, we should get to know each other better. *(reason/cause)*
while	**While** the Trans were on vacation, their house was robbed. *(time)*
	My little sister loves vegetables, **while** most children dislike them. *(contrast)*

> **TIP**
>
> Good writers end sentences with the clause that most logically leads to the idea in the next sentence. Think about the flow or coherence of your ideas as you edit, especially with complex sentences.

SELF CHECK

Correct the errors in adverb clauses.

1. Amy had so good time at the party that she didn't want to leave.

2. Although Ana Marie was sick, she didn't come to the party.

3. Even though the pool is warm, but we decided not to go swimming.

4. Mitchell has to graduate at the end of this year because of he is running out of money for tuition.

5. Despite the fact that my sister spent hours writing her essay she received a failing grade on it.

EDITING PRACTICE

1 *Put a check (✓) next to the sentences that use adverb clauses correctly. Correct the sentences that have errors.*

_____ 1. Because the class didn't agree with the teacher's grading system, we had to abide by it.

_____ 2. Even though Jane doesn't like the sweater her grandmother gave her she wears it often.

_____ 3. They sold the piano despite the fact that it had sentimental value.

_____ 4. Since I live across the street from school and eat all my meals on campus.

_____ 5. Dr. Dubus prefers to travel by train, while most people prefer to fly nowadays.

_____ 6. My dad turned on the air conditioner because the temperature was approaching 100°F.

_____ 7. We read that book last semester though it was a requirement of the course.

_____ 8. Because Camille finished the project on time, she stayed up past midnight working on it.

_____ 9. Although the price of electricity is increasing, but we continue to consume more and more of it.

_____10. People show so little respect to the elderly that many people fear growing old.

_____11. Due to the fact that the fattening dorm food, Gilbert gained ten pounds last semester.

_____12. I need to get some new keys even though I lost mine.

2 *Read the following paragraph. Complete the paragraph with the correct subordinating conjunction.*

      Last summer I bought an old Vespa motor scooter and restored it to its original condition. I almost did not begin this project because I was _____ shocked at the price of thirty-year-

1. so / such
old scooters that I almost didn't buy mine. _____ I found my scooter, I had looked at

2. While / Before
dozens of others. Although mine needed a lot of work, _____ I chose my particular

3. even though / ø
Vespa _____ its year and model are considered the peak of Vespa design.

4. since / even though
_____ I was restoring my Vespa over the summer, I went to scooter shows and shops

5. While / Although
and met a lot of nice people who were also scooter enthusiasts. _____ I met these

6. Though / Since
people, I have joined the Vespa Club, gone on several rallies, and made many new friends. Who would have thought a scooter could influence a person's life so much. I don't think I will ever sell my scooter _____ I could lose touch with the interesting people I have met. Other

7. because / though
people may soon share my enthusiasm for scooters _____ the Vespa

8. due to the fact that / due to

company is beginning to sell new Vespas in the United States again. _____ you see

9. Until / Wherever

Vespas for sale, you should take one for a test drive _____ you too can experience the

10. Ø / so that

fun of riding a scooter.

3 *In the following paragraphs, ten words or phrases are underlined. In six places, either the underlined item or the following adverb clause is wrong. Correct each error.*

The importance of language is obvious yet mysterious. On the surface, language allows

people to communicate, but it also holds a people's culture, values, and ideals together. **(1)** <u>When</u>

a group of people loses or begins to lose its language, more than just a tool of communication is

lost. One example of this is **(2)** <u>whenever</u> Korea was declared a protectorate and annexed as a

Japanese colony after the Japanese-Korean War. Koreans were forbidden to use the Korean

language in schools and public areas. Even though the Korean language prevailed, **(3)** <u>but</u> Koreans

were set apart from each other **(4)** <u>because of</u> they could no longer use their own language.

(5) <u>Wherever</u> colonization has taken place throughout the world, we can observe this same

phenomenon.

Languages are not always lost as a result of colonization or physical domination. **(6)** <u>Due</u>

<u>to</u> English is becoming so popular, many languages are currently fighting to survive. People who

live in countries with small populations are forced to speak English **(7)** <u>so that</u> they can

communicate with the outside world. The people of Wales are a perfect example of this. Welsh is

spoken by **(8)** <u>so</u> a small number of people <u>that</u> it was on the verge of extinction. **(9)** <u>As soon as</u> the

Welsh realized that they might lose their language, they began to try to save it. **(10)** <u>Because</u>

language holds so much cultural significance. It is vital that all languages, no matter how small,

are kept alive.

4 *The following paragraph has ten errors in the use of adverb clauses, including punctuation. Find and correct the errors.*

In the short story "The Catbird Seat," James Thurber, the author, uses humor to illustrate the

war between the sexes. Mr. Martin and Mrs. Barrows are introduced at the beginning of the story,

and we immediately see Mr. Martin's intense anger toward his coworker. Mr. Martin is a boring man who is used to a strict routine as soon as Mrs. Barrows is just the opposite. Wherever Mrs. Barrows goes, change follows. Mr. Martin feels her main goal is to disrupt and ruin his life. Although Mrs. Barrows has a strong personality, and a battle between the two follows. In order that Mrs. Barrows doesn't realize it, she has alienated herself from all of her coworkers, especially Mr. Martin. Mr. Martin is so upset that he decides his only option is to murder Mrs. Barrows. Before Mr. Martin decides to commit murder he has never broken his daily routine of work, dinner, and two glasses of milk before bed. Even though Mr. Martin's decision goes against his nature, but he feels there is no other solution. Unless he comes up with a better plan. Mr. Martin is going to follow through with his murder scheme. Fortunately, the murder scheme fails, and Mr. Martin's new plan for getting rid of Mrs. Barrows is better than murder, until it is still not completely honest. Mr. Martin feels that Mrs. Barrows is such despicable that his actions are justified. Despite the fact that Mrs. Barrows is a difficult person, she has good intentions. Mr. Martin fails to see this side of her personality because of he is so scared that his precious routine will be destroyed. Mr. Martin's routine is restored as soon as Mrs. Barrows leaves the company. Overall, this is a humorous story. Although it is a shame that in the classic battle between the sexes, strong women are so often portrayed in a negative light.

WRITING TOPICS

Choose one of the topics below, and write at least one paragraph. Be sure to use adverb clauses. After you complete your first draft, concentrate on editing your work. Keep in mind the editing practice from this chapter.

1. Although the roles of men and women in society are changing, each is still governed by traditional rules and expectations. Compare the traditional male and female roles in two countries. Contrast traditional male/female roles with the more modern rules and expectations that men and women face today.

2. Explain how our mental health and physical health are affected by our daily habits and lifestyle choices. Describe how people feel and look when they have healthy habits versus unhealthy habits.

Go to page 106 for more practice with adverb clauses.

CHAPTER 8

Conditionals

PRETEST

*Check your understanding of conditional sentences. Put a check (✓)
next to the sentences that are correct.*

_____ 1. If Joaquin buys a new car, he gets an SUV.

_____ 2. The skiing is always good if the mountains get a lot of snow.

_____ 3. Daniel has always been a bad driver, and nobody ever wants
to ride in his car. If he begins to drive better, we will feel safer
in his car.

_____ 4. Studies show that if people exercised daily, they will feel better.

_____ 5. If the two variables are equal and show the result that is
expected.

_____ 6. I would volunteer at a homeless shelter if I have more time.

_____ 7. If we had invested in the stock market earlier, we would be
better off today.

_____ 8. If Eddy and Melinda try out for the play, they will definitely
be selected for the leading roles.

_____ 9. If I were you, I will move to Hawaii and live near the beach.

_____10. The mayor would have had our support if he had changed his
stance on the environment.

EDITING FOCUS

Conditional sentences allow a writer to describe cause-and-effect relationships, to show possibility in the future, and to rethink the past. There are four basic patterns of conditional sentences. Each pattern has a different combination of verb forms. As writer and editor of your work, you must be able to form conditional sentences correctly in order to convey the meaning you want.

FORMING CONDITIONALS

1. A conditional sentence has an *if* clause (adverb clause) and a result clause (independent clause). The *if* clause shows the necessary condition for the particular result.

   adverb clause   independent clause
   If I train hard, I can finish the race.

        independent clause   adverb clause
   My father will start a fire in the fireplace *if* it rains.

2. A conditional clause, like any other adverb clause used alone, is a fragment. It must be attached to an independent clause.

Complete sentence	**If we studied more**, we would get better grades.
Fragment	**If** we studied more.
Complete sentence	Coco and I don't want to go sailing **if it is too windy.**
Fragment	**If** it is too windy.

3. The *if* clause can come before or after the independent clause; however, the punctuation is different. When a sentence begins with an *if* clause, the clause is followed by a comma. When the *if* clause comes second, no comma is required.

Comma	**If she decides to be a teacher**, she will have a small salary.
No comma	She will have a small salary **if she decides to be a teacher.**
Comma	**If you had done your homework**, you could go out with us now.
No comma	You could go out with us now **if you had done your homework.**

4. In addition to *if*, conjunctions such as *unless* and *even if* are used in conditional sentences.

   Unless it rains, the dance will be held outside.

   We are going on our trip **even if** it snows.

USING CONDITIONALS

1. Use conditional sentences to show cause-and-effect relationships. The *if* clause shows a condition or cause, and the independent clause shows the result or effect.

condition

result

If I don't get good grades, I won't get a car for my eighteenth birthday.

result

condition

We wouldn't have to conserve water *if* we lived in a rainy climate.

2. Conditional sentences indicate real and hypothetical (untrue) situations. The verb tense in each clause shows whether the situation is real or hypothetical.

REAL OR FACTUAL CONDITIONALS IN THE PRESENT OR FUTURE

In real conditionals, which are about real ideas or situations in the present or future, the simple present is used in the *if* clause. The verb tense used in the result clause depends on the idea or situation.

- For habitual actions or situations, use the simple present in the result clause.

  If I don't **write** my shopping list down, I always **forget** something at the store.

- For a predictable fact or general truth, use either the simple present or the simple future in the result clause.

  If it **rains,** the company usually **postpones** the picnic.

  If the temperature **falls** below 32° F, the roads **will freeze**.

NOTE: *When* or *whenever* can replace *if* in conditional sentences that express habitual actions, predictable facts, or general truths.

  My family loves to have a fire in the fireplace **whenever it rains**.

  When it snows hard, the schools close.

  When the temperature rises above 32° F, the snow will melt.

- To express an action or situation in the future, use the simple future in the result clause.

  If I don't **wake up** early tomorrow, I **will be** late for work again.

- To express ideas like ability, necessity, predictions, or possibility in a conditional sentence, use modals or phrasal modals in the result clause.

  If it **rains,** we **should cancel** the picnic.

  If the storm **continues,** the plane **won't be able** to take off.

HYPOTHETICAL CONDITIONALS IN THE PRESENT OR FUTURE

- To write about hypothetical, imaginary, or impossible situations in the present or future, use the simple past in the *if* clause and *would* + the base form of the verb in the result clause. *Could* can also be used in the result clause to express a possible option.

If my parents were here, they would help us.
(In truth, my parents are not here, so they cannot help us.)

If I had a million dollars, I would quit my job.
(In truth, I don't have a million dollars, so I won't quit my job.)

If I had a million dollars, I could quit my job. *(Could = would be able to)*

NOTE: *Were* is used for both singular and plural subjects in formal writing. *Was* may be used informally, but it is not considered the best choice for formal writing.

If she were a little taller, she would be taller than her father.

- Hypothetical conditionals can also be used to make a suggestion. In the following example, the writer is suggesting that the listener work less so that he or she can spend more time studying.

If I were you, I would study more and work less.

HYPOTHETICAL CONDITIONALS IN THE PAST

- To write about hypothetical, imaginary, or impossible situations in the past, use the past perfect in the *if* clause, and *would + have* + past participle in the result clause. The situations in these conditional sentences did not happen. *Would* expresses a desired or predictable result. *Could* and *might* can also be used in the result clause to express a possibility.

If I had graduated last June, I would have moved from this apartment.
(I didn't graduate in June, so I didn't move.)

If I hadn't been late for the interview, I could have gotten the job.
(Could have gotten = would have been able to get)

MIXED HYPOTHETICAL CONDITIONALS

- Use a mixed hypothetical conditional to write about an untrue condition in the past with an untrue result in the present.

past perfect · would + verb

If he had written a best-selling novel, he would be famous now.

(He didn't write a best-selling novel, so he is not famous.)

- Use a mixed hypothetical conditional to write about an untrue condition in the present with an untrue result in the past.

simple past · would + have + past participle

If I had a car, I would have taken you to school.

(I don't have a car, so I couldn't have taken you to school.)

3. The subordinating conjunction *unless* means *if . . . not.*

We will live in Barcelona unless our plans change.
(We will live in Barcelona if our plans do not change.)

I always finish my homework unless I get interrupted by my little sister.
(I always finish my homework if I do not get interrupted by my little sister.)

4. The subordinating conjunctions *whether or not* and *even if* mean the condition does not affect the result.

result | condition
Adrian is going to change her major whether or not her parents agree.

(Adrian will change her major. It doesn't matter what her parents think.)

condition | result
Even if we are not finished, we have to turn in the test in one hour.

(We have to turn in the test in one hour. It doesn't matter if we finish or not.)

5. Modals other than *would* are frequently used in conditional sentences. They express meanings such as possibility, ability, advice, and necessity.

Real conditional	If we fly a long distance, my daughter **may sleep** for part of the flight.
Predictive conditional	If roses are planted in the winter, they **should bloom** the next spring.
Present/future hypothetical conditional	If we took the high-speed train, we **could arrive** in as few as two hours.
Past hypothetical conditional	If Sasha had practiced more, **she might have been** a concert cellist.

6. Additional results of a previously mentioned condition often show up in later sentences of a paragraph. In most cases, these results require the use of a modal such as *would*.

   If Mary Ann got financial support, she would go to dental school. She **would like** to be a dentist, but the tuition is too high for her.

> **TIP**
>
> Scan your writing for the subordinating conjunctions *if, unless,* and *even if*. When you see one of these words, circle it, and review the rules for conditional sentences. Check that the verb phrase is correct in both clauses.

SELF CHECK

Correct the errors involving conditionals.

1. If I drive to school, I would be on time for class.

2. If Mrs. Candelaria teaches the class again, she will assign fewer essays. She would also do some other things differently.

3. If Julie were invited to go horseback riding after class yesterday, she would have gone.

4. If I was you, I would buy a new car.

5. If the sun had risen earlier, Mr. Gupta would meditate on the beach this morning.

EDITING PRACTICE

1 *Put a check (✓) next to the sentences that use conditionals correctly. Correct the sentences that have errors in structure and/or meaning.*

____ 1. It would hurt Rudy's feelings if his friends tell secrets behind his back.

____ 2. If I were the queen of England, I would wear a crown of diamonds.

____ 3. When I wait patiently, I will get what I want.

____ 4. If Mr. Canon had a pet, he would be happier than he is now because he will have companionship.

____ 5. Traditions are difficult to maintain. If people don't keep their families together.

____ 6. Dr. Ashcroft would be my favorite professor, if he had given me an A on the term paper.

____ 7. We eat dinner at home unless my mother doesn't want to cook.

____ 8. If parents communicated well with their children, both parents and children will be happy and feel better about each other.

____ 9. Mrs. Steele would be a school principal if she had taken the time to get the credentials.

____10. If Bernice goes to the concert, she would hear a lot of songs that she knows.

____11. If my car insurance had gone down, I could have bought a new car.

____12. Congress is going to raise taxes even if the voters are against it.

2 *Read the following paragraph. Complete the paragraph with the correct choice in each conditional sentence.*

As an urban planning student, someday I hope to make life easier for people living in metropolitan areas by improving parklands, public transportation, and community meeting areas. If I could design an ideal city, I _____ on these three important
1. would focus / will focus
aspects of city life first. If it _____ possible, the city would have sufficient open land
2. was / were
surrounding it for hiking, fishing, picnicing, and other outdoor activities. The city charter

_____ that this land could never be developed. If the city were large, I
3. will mandate / would mandate
_____ a safe and efficient subway system. This system _____
4. would design / had designed   _5. will be / would be_
underground and nonpolluting; therefore, it would be only a benefit to the citizens and not a

burden in any way. I would also spend a great deal of time designing appealing, fun, and

educational community areas that _____ all citizens from the youngest to the
6. attract / would attract

oldest. If the city _____ sufficient money to spend on community meeting areas, I would
7. had / has

like to see museums, schools, and parks that host concerts and classes. In any city, if people have

access to parks, to safe and efficient public transportation, and to a feeling of community, they

_____ content in their place of residence. Urban planners know this now, but if
8. will be / would be

they had realized it earlier, we _____ as much urban decay today as
9. would not have had / would not have

we do. It is my dream to create peaceful cities and happy citizens, and if I _____
10. graduated / graduate

on time, I will be able to begin my dream in two years.

3 *In the following paragraph, five of the underlined verbs have errors while the others do not.*
Write the correct conditional form above each verb with an error.

If I (1) were faced with a life-threatening or altering challenge, I (2) would make some

changes in my life. First, if I (3) were about to die, I (4) will look back over my life. If I (5) have the

time and opportunity, I (6) would travel to Europe and Asia. I (7) would probably want to do as

many things as I could because I (8) would not have much time left on Earth. If I (9) had a disease

that (10) will affect other people, then I (11) will have to stay away from them and seek medical

help. When I looked back on my life, I (12)) would see if there (13) were any bad deeds that I had

done and I would try to make up for them. Fortunately, I am not facing a life-threatening

challenge, but just the thought of this makes me want to critically evaluate my life and how I am

living it. If I (14) realize that I am making mistakes now, I (15) change them before it is too late.

4 *The following paragraph has ten errors in the use of conditional sentences. Find and correct*
the errors.

If you wanted to save money and achieve some peace in your life, try planting a vegetable

garden. Saving money and achieving peace are seemingly unrelated goals; however, both are

surprisingly attainable by planting a garden. If you knew the price of seeds, you can understand

how inexpensive it is to grow an entire vegetable garden yourself. If you have ever found joy in

growing a plant, you will understand how it is possible to find peace in planting. If you had a

small plot of land, it will be easier to begin your garden; however, a lot of land isn't necessary.

Even if all you have is a small patio with a few containers, you still succeed in growing vegetables if you do the following. First, it is important to have good soil. If you composted your garbage, you already have the perfect fertilizer for your garden. If you don't, it is possible to find good fertilizers at any nursery. Next, it's time to decide which vegetables to plant. This depends on the time of year. If it was the cool season, vegetables such as broccoli, lettuce, and onions will do well. Summer vegetables like tomatoes, cucumbers, and corn would grow well if it's warmer. Depending on the plant, you may begin harvesting in as soon as four weeks. One downside to be aware of is pests. Whenever you had planted your vegetables, you will have to be aware of vegetable-eating bugs. Try planting a vegetable garden any time of year, and see what you save financially and gain spiritually. Hopefully, at some point in the future you will say to yourself, "If only I had known the benefits of a vegetable garden earlier, I would save so much money and find enjoyment so much sooner."

WRITING TOPICS

Choose one of the topics below, and write at least one paragraph. Be sure to use conditional sentences. After you complete your first draft, concentrate on editing your work. Keep in mind the editing practice from this chapter.

1. Describe one problem that exists in the world today. This can be a global problem or a problem that involves only you. If you could solve this problem, how would you do it? If you solved the problem, how would the world or your life change? If this problem had never existed, how would our world or your life have been different?

2. Because you have been studying the English language for many years, you probably have opinions on the best way to learn a new language. If someone wanted to learn your first language, how would you teach him or her? What techniques did you find helpful while learning English that you would use as a teacher of your language? What could someone learn about the customs and culture of your country if you taught them your native language?

Go to pages 105 and 106 for more practice with conditionals.

CHAPTER 9

Noun Clauses

PRETEST

Check your understanding of noun clauses. Put a check (✓) next to the sentences that are correct.

____ 1. The judge informed the lawyer that the defendant was out of order.

____ 2. The lawyer responded that she would try to control her client.

____ 3. Whales migrate south to Mexico in the winter has created a tourist industry there.

____ 4. Is Ramon at home? I don't know where Ramon is home.

____ 5. We don't know what time is it.

____ 6. It is necessary that Bo gets home before midnight or her parents will be furious.

____ 7. A nutritionist recommended me to eat less.

____ 8. Nari advised that her assistant learn more computer skills.

____ 9. Naomi told me James is still in the library.

____10. The teacher said that water froze at 32° F.

EDITING FOCUS

Noun clauses are used in the same way as nouns: as subjects or objects of verbs, as complements, and as objects of prepositions. They are also used in reported, or indirect speech to express a person's thoughts or ideas. As a writer and editor, it is important to know how to form and use noun clauses correctly. Notice how noun clauses are used in the following two sentences.

subject   verb

What the professor says in class will definitely be on the next quiz.

subject verb   object

We can't believe that New Zealand has more sheep than people.

FORMING NOUN CLAUSES

1. A noun clause begins with either *that, if,* or a *wh-* word. A noun clause can appear at the beginning, in the middle, or at the end of a sentence.

that	**That they live at opposite ends of the state** makes their relationship difficult.
	The reason (that) the delivery is late is the snowstorm in Toronto.
	The students knew **(that) they were late for class.**
what	**What we love to cook** is spicy Thai food.
when	We don't know **when the teacher will give the next quiz.**
where	**Where I left my cell phone** is a mystery.
why	It is unclear **why you lied to your parents.**
how	I cannot believe **how much homework the instructor gave.**
whether/if	Tanya doesn't know **whether or not she will have a graduation party.**

NOTE: *Whether or not* or *if* can be used for sentences that answer indirect yes/no questions.

We're not sure **if Gabriel wants to go to the concert tonight.**

We're not certain **whether or not we can get tickets.**

OR

We're not certain **whether we can get tickets or not.**

2. The word *that* can be omitted at the beginning of a noun clause if the noun clause is the object or complement of the sentence.

His teacher thinks **(that) Samir is a good student.**

It seems **(that) there won't be any more tests this term.**

The word *that* cannot be omitted when the noun clause is the subject of the sentence.

That he is a good student is obvious.

NOT
He is a good student is obvious.

Very often the word *it* functions as the subject, and the noun clause comes at the end of the sentence.

***It* is obvious (that) he is a good student.**

3. Noun clauses that function as subjects use a singular verb.

Why Jonathan did not complete the semester **is** unclear.

That the answer was not correct **was** clear.

4. Noun clauses use statement word order, not question word order. The auxiliaries *do, does,* and *did* are not used in noun clauses.

Will is wondering where his roommate is.

NOT
Will is wondering where is his roommate.

Why Carmen changed her name is unclear to her parents.

NOT
Why did Carmen change her name is unclear to her parents.

5. Use the base form of the verb after adjectives or verbs of urgency or request. Third-person singular subjects of the noun clause (*he, she,* and *it*) also use the base form.

Adjectives of urgency	*critical, crucial, desirable, essential, imperative, important, necessary, urgent, vital*
	It is *essential* (that) Marco attend the meeting. adjective of urgency subject base verb
	It is *urgent* that I leave early today
Adjectives of request	*best, recommended*
	It is *recommended* (that) you take the introductory class first.
	It is *best* (that) the medicine be taken every two hours.
Verbs of urgency	*command, demand, insist, order, urge*
	Seon's parents *insisted* (that) he be home by midnight.
	Peter *insisted* (that) we not leave late.
Verbs of request or suggestion	*advise, ask, prefer, propose, recommend, request, suggest*
	My counselor *suggested* (that) I not take more than fifteen units next term.

USING NOUN CLAUSES

Noun clauses using *that* commonly follow a number of verbs, adjectives, and expressions.

Verbs

assume	fear	learn	recognize
agree	feel	notice	regret
believe	figure out	observe	remember
care	find out	predict	reveal
conclude	forget	presume	show
decide	hear	pretend	suppose
demonstrate	hope	prove	suspect
discover	imagine	read	teach
doubt	indicate	realize	think
dream	know	recall	understand

Research indicates *(that) the current economic trend will continue.*

We understand *(that) the flight may be postponed.*

Adjectives

afraid	disappointed/ing	proud
amazed/ing	fortunate	shocked/ing
angry	furious	sorry
ashamed	happy	sure
astounded/ing	horrified/ing	surprised/ing
aware	impossible	strange
certain	lucky	terrified/ing
clear	obvious	thrilled/ing
convinced/ing	pleased/ing	true
delighted/ful	positive	worried

The university is shocked *(that) student enrollment keeps rising.*

It is fortunate *(that) the results support the same conclusion.*

Expressions

The effect that
The fact that
The idea that
The possibility that
The reason that
The way that

The idea *(that) some languages are harder than others* **is a myth.**

The possibility *(that) the senator will be reelected* **is small.**

SELF CHECK 1

Correct the errors involving noun clauses.

1. Talal is wondering where is his roommate.

2. What we love to eat are Italian food.

3. When they traditionally do in Australia is have picnics or barbecues on big holidays.

4. Why is Flight 109 delayed cannot be explained.

5. It is important that Mr. Lee primarily uses an English-only dictionary in class.

USING NOUN CLAUSES IN REPORTED/INDIRECT SPEECH

1. Noun clauses are used to report your own or someone else's thoughts, ideas, or words.

   I told the actress (that) her character had always been my favorite in the television series.

   Mrs. Mahini said (that) many of her students do volunteer work in the community.

   We asked the policeman where the nearest gas station was.

2. Verb tense, adverbs, and pronouns change in reported speech.

Direct Speech/Quotation	Reported/Indirect Speech	Comments
Marina said, "I cannot come over to your house because I have to study for a test tomorrow."	Marina said (that) she could not come over to my house because she had to study for a test the next day.	When the verb in the quotation is in the present, it generally changes to the past in reported speech. When changing from a quotation to reported speech, notice how pronouns and possessive adjectives change.

(continued page 84)

Direct Speech/Quotation	Reported/Indirect Speech	Comments
Bob said, "I went hiking last week."	Bob said (that) he **had gone** hiking last week.	When the verb in the quotation is in the simple past, it generally changes to the past perfect in reported speech.
Kareem said, "Organic chemistry is the hardest class that I **have ever taken.**"	Kareem said (that) organic chemistry is the hardest class that he **has ever taken.**	Reported speech may be in the present tense, if the statement is still true, if the statement is a fact or scientific truth, or if the statement was just reported.
Mr. Cruz told the class, "Mount Everest **is called** Chomo-Lungma by the Tibetans."	Mr. Cruz told the class (that) Mount Everest **is called** Chomo-Lungma by the Tibetans.	
Ryan said, "I am happy with my grades."	Ryan said (that) he is happy with his grades.	
Every day the professor says, "Class participation **counts** in your final grades for the course."	Every day the professor says (that) class participation **counts** in our final grades for the course.	Reporting verbs are generally in the past; however, when the reporting verb is in the present, the verb in reported speech remains in the present.

3. Use the following verbs to report other people's thoughts, ideas, or words.

Stating verbs   *acknowledge, add, advise, announce, argue, assert, believe, caution, claim, command, declare, demand, deny, explain, indicate, inform, maintain, mention, notify, order, remark, report, say, state, suggest, tell, urge, warn, write*

The ambassador **stated** *(that) the negotiations were progressing well.*

The instructor **announced** to the class *(that) scores below 74 percent were non-passing.*

The environmentalist **argued** *(that) global warming would eventually kill the Earth.*

NOTE: The listener (a noun or pronoun) must follow the verb *tell*. Do not use *to* after *tell*.

My boss told me that I could expect a promotion within the next year.

NOT

My boss told to me that I could expect a promotion within the next year.

Mentioning the listener is not necessary with the verb *say*; however, if you mention the listener, you must use *say to*.

Every day our English teacher says (to the class) how important good grammar is.

Questioning verbs	*ask, inquire, question, wonder*
	The students **asked** *where the lab would be.*
Responding verbs	*agree, answer, concur, disagree, dispute, reply, respond*
	The industrialist **replied** *(that) global warming was an issue under discussion.*
Concluding verbs	*conclude, realize*
	The author **concluded** *(that) the issue would require further investigation.*

TIP

Vary the length of the sentences you write. During the editing process, look for a combination of simple sentences and complex sentences with adverb, noun, and adjective clauses. A short sentence can be very effective if it is used after several long complex sentences.

4. Time and place words change in reported speech.

Direct Speech	Reported/Indirect Speech
now	then, at that time
today	that day
tomorrow	the next/following day, a day later
tonight	that night
yesterday	the day before, the previous day
yet	by that time
last week/month/year	the week/month/year before, the previous week/month/year
this week/month/year	that week/month/year
next week/month/year	the next/following week/month/year
this	that
these	those
here	there

Direct	Florence asked, "Why is the moon so bright **tonight?**"
Reported	Florence asked why the moon was so bright **that night**.
Direct	Tomo said, "I cannot study **here** today because there is too much noise."
Reported	Tomo said (that) he couldn't study **there** that day because there was too much noise.

5. Certain modals also change in reported speech.

Direct Speech	**Reported Speech**
will	would
can	could
may	might
must	had to

Direct	Afshin said, "I will never be able to spell well in English."
Reported	Afshin said (that) he would never be able to spell well in English.
Direct	"You may not be able to buy tickets until tomorrow," said Marilyn.
Reported	Marilyn said (that) we might not be able to buy tickets until the next day.

SELF CHECK 2

Correct the errors involving reported speech.

1. The receptionist told to me that Professor Romy was not holding office hours today.

2. My boss asked me what had I learned at the conference.

3. My roommate's father asked me why aren't you in class.

4. At 8:00 this morning, the professor told the student to begin the exam now.

5. When we were at Pietro's house, he claimed that the mess here was unusual.

EDITING PRACTICE

1. *Put a check (✓) next to the sentences that use noun clauses correctly. Correct the sentences that have errors.*

____ 1. Education prepares people for what will they face in the real world.

____ 2. It is true everyone makes mistakes in life.

____ 3. The coach told Seon how he could improve his tennis game.

____ 4. After the burglary, the police recommended that she keeps her jewelry in a safe.

_____ 5. Alice forgot how she had used oxygen or not in the experiment to get the current results.

_____ 6. Ralph said that he was afraid that he will be late for his next class.

_____ 7. Community involvement has taught me that everyone has to contribute in order to make our environment livable.

_____ 8. Maria wondered if she can catch the 6:35 train even though it was almost 6:30.

_____ 9. The nurse said the new mother that she should put the baby on a feeding schedule immediately.

_____ 10. The growing world population is causing environmental problems is troubling.

_____ 11. We saw our final grades and feel they are fair.

_____ 12. Consumer advocates maintain that the auto industry must take some responsibility for the country's smog problems.

_____ 13. What does she loves is Indian food.

_____ 14. How teenagers create slang are an area of study at the university.

2 *Read the following paragraph. Complete the paragraph with the correct noun clause.*

Maturity is a state that most adolescents and teenagers hope to reach because of the

freedom that comes with it. _____ know a child has reached maturity

1. How parents / How do parents

depends on the child's level of responsibility, not simply age. Some physical signs of maturity

occur _____ voice begin to get deeper or _____

2. when a boy's / when does a boy's   **3. when does he start / when he starts**

to grow a beard. However, _____ look for is a sign of social development

4. what do parents / what parents

before they feel their child is mature and deserves more freedom. When parents decide

_____ deserves some of the freedom that comes with age, that child

5. that their child / why their child

finally feels mature. Most teens say _____ staying out later at night, driving a car, and dating

6. if / that

are some hoped-for freedoms that come with maturity. _____ most of these changes

7. When / That

come gradually makes them difficult to notice at first but nevertheless significant. Some teens

figure out _____ mature when an activity that was once considered fun is no

8. that they are / are they

longer so much fun. Playing in the freezing snow for hours, riding skateboards, and trading

baseball cards are priorities for children, but with maturity these activities lose some of their

appeal. When life changes and we realize _____ we are adults, it becomes critical

9. where / that

_____ clean clothes, food in the refrigerator, and a neat room. It is obvious

10. that one has / that one have

_____ physical maturity is inevitable, but we can only hope _____ emotional

11. if / that   **12. that / for**

maturity comes along with it.

3 *In the following paragraph, five of the underlined clauses have errors. Write your corrections above each underlined clause.*

It has been said (1) <u>that the United States is the land of second chances</u>. It is true (2) <u>that American society is eager to help</u> those who have made mistakes or are seeking new opportunities by providing them with a second chance to succeed. The juvenile justice system is an excellent example of (3) <u>how can mistakes be erased</u>. Every state in the country has programs for dependent, neglected, or delinquent children. This system is based on the belief (4) <u>that the state has the moral responsibility to act as a type of parent to all children in need of protection</u>. It encourages the idea (5) <u>what juveniles should be given a second chance</u>. The community college system is another example of a second chance that society offers. Adults are encouraged to return to school to learn new skills, and teenagers are able to improve their high school GPAs in order to go on to universities. Community college mission statements often declare (6) <u>that increasing educational opportunities for all is a primary goal</u>. (7) <u>That the community college system admits anyone over 18 years of age</u> shows its willingness to provide a second chance to all. Many immigrants look at a new life in the United States as a second chance to improve their lives and the lives of their children. Famous and influential immigrants have said (8) <u>that they will not have had the opportunity to excel in their home countries</u>. (9) <u>How do people choose to use their second chances</u> is never certain. (10) <u>The truth is when some take advantage of a second chance</u>, while others squander it and continue to make the same mistakes. However, one of the strongest beliefs in the United States is (11) <u>that people deserve the chance to succeed even if they initially fail</u>.

4 *The following essay has ten errors in the use of noun clauses. Find and correct the errors.*

The famous generation gap between young people and their parents that was so apparent in the 1960s still exists today. It is said that the generation gap is a division between two generations, generally young people and their parents. When parents and children discover they have little in common, the gap has begun to form. Young people maintain that their parents don't understand them, worry too much, and restrict their freedom. The parents respond that their children don't respect them, watch too much television, and want too much freedom at an early age. In other words, what children and parents respect are vastly different. What are the reasons for this lack of understanding is hard to say, but there are a few theories.

In previous decades, parents have said that the generation gap developed from young people challenging their parent's old-fashioned ideals and beliefs; however, in the technological twenty-first century, old and young generations have said that they are separated by different skills and abilities. These challenges are true for all families, but for immigrant families the problem may be more serious. The older generation tells to its children that they have lost all sense of tradition and culture. What do the children learn to value in their new culture is not the same as what do their traditional parents value.

Children of earlier generations have sworn that they will not let this happen in their families, yet the gap has continued to exist. That a lack of communication and respect is causing their children to drift farther and farther from them are shocking to this generation of parents. In order to slow the formation of the generation gap, it is vital that a child listens to his or her parents. In addition, counselors suggest that parents are available to listen to their children at all times. Many families don't know what they will be able to heal the gap between the generations, but young people and their parents must still try.

> **TIP**
>
> Take advantage of your instructor's knowledge of English. Meet with him or her often for comments and suggestions on your writing.

WRITING TOPICS

Choose one of the topics below, and write at least one paragraph. Be sure to use noun clauses. After you complete your first draft, concentrate on editing your work. Keep in mind the editing practice from this chapter.

1. Some superstitions you may be familiar with are "Don't let a black cat cross your path" and "If you break a mirror, you will have seven years of bad luck." What other superstitions do you know? What culture or country are they from? How do you think these superstitions developed? Do you or does anyone you know believe in them?

2. Describe the person whom you admire most in the world. This can be a world figure or someone closer to home, such as a parent or neighbor. Explain what this person has done to deserve your admiration.

Go to page 106 for more practice with noun clauses.

CHAPTER 10

Word Order

- - - - - - - - - - - - - - - - - - -

- - - - - - - - - - - - - - - - - - -

- - - - - - - - - - - - - - - - - - -

- - - - - - - - - - - - - - - - - - -

- - - - - - - - - - - - - - - - - - -

- - - - - - - - - - - - - - - - - - -

PRETEST

Check your understanding of word order. Put a check (✓) next to the sentences that are correct.

____ 1. I don't think I turned the iron off.

____ 2. We get the bus off at the next stop.

____ 3. He didn't tell me where is the car parked.

____ 4. Charlotte just bought a long blue prom dress.

____ 5. Especially Italian ice cream is good.

____ 6. I wonder if Rick has done his homework.

____ 7. George and Lance last Saturday went to the video arcade all day.

____ 8. The two-story brick house almost burned down last night that is on the corner.

____ 9. The librarian is reading to the children a story.

____ 10. Are Charles and Judith at the movies?

EDITING FOCUS

In English there are rules that determine the order of words in sentences. If these rules are not followed, word order errors occur. These errors can be serious and change the meaning of a sentence or cause the reader to misunderstand. Other times, word order errors can be less serious and simply lead to an awkward sentence. It is important for writers to use correct word order and to know which types of word order errors to edit for.

In the following examples, notice the difference in meaning depending on where the adverb *only* is placed in the sentence.

> **Only** Mary knows how to fix the VCR.
> *(No one else knows how to fix it.)*

> Mary knows how to fix *only* the VCR.
> *(She knows how to fix the VCR, but nothing else.)*

FORMING SENTENCES WITH CORRECT WORD ORDER

1. For statements, the basic word order in English is (A) *subject + verb + object* or (B) *subject + verb + complement.*

	S	V	O		S	V	C

   (A) The tourists are studying a map.   **(B) The tourists are lost.**

2. Word order changes for questions. The verb or auxiliary *be* or another auxiliary verb—*do/does/did/have/has,* or a modal—comes before the subject to form *yes/no* and *wh-* questions.

Mr. Ho likes to play chess.	**Does** Mr. Ho like to play chess?
Mr. Ho was a chess champion.	**Was** Mr. Ho a chess champion?
Mr. Ho has entered many tournaments.	**Has** Mr. Ho entered many tournaments?
Mr. Ho is entering a chess tournament soon.	When **is** Mr. Ho entering a chess tournament?
Mr. Ho will be finished soon.	**Will** Mr. Ho be finished soon?
Mr. Ho should practice in the library.	Where **should** Mr. Ho practice?

3. Indirect questions use statement word order. Indirect questions are noun clauses that are included within a sentence. (See Chapter 9)

Basic question	Does the supermarket stay open 24 hours?
Indirect question	Alexi wonders **if the supermarket stays open 24 hours.**
Basic question	Where is the 24-hour market?
Indirect question	Do you know **where the 24-hour market is?**

4. When a verb takes both a direct and indirect object, the word order generally follows two patterns.

Subject + Verb	Indirect Object	Direct Object	Indirect Object
(A) The manager gave	Cara	a raise.	
(B) The manager gave		a raise	to Cara.

NOTE: In pattern B, most verbs take the preposition *to;* however, some take the preposition *for.*

Verbs that use the preposition *to* include: *bring, give, hand, lend, mail, offer, pass, read, sell, send, serve, show, teach, tell, throw,* and *toss.* Verbs that use the preposition *for* include: *build, buy, cook, find, leave, make, order,* and *save.* Verbs that use both prepositions *to* and *for* include: *do, get, pay, sing, take,* and *write.*

5. Verbs such as *hand in, call back,* and *pick up* are called phrasal verbs or two-word verbs. These verbs consist of a verb and one or more particles. Particles look like prepositions, but they change the meaning of the verb. Two-word verbs are either separable or nonseparable.

- **Separable two-word verbs:**

    Jamie **handed in** his homework.

    Jamie **handed** his homework **in**.

With these verbs, a noun can come after the two-word verb or between the verb and the preposition. A pronoun must always come between the verb and the preposition.

    Dr. Finder **picked up** the package.

    Dr. Finder **picked it up.**

    NOT
    Dr. Finder picked up it.

Some separable two-word verbs include: *ask out, call back, call off, call up, cross out, do over, figure out, fill in, fill out, fill up, find out, give back, give up, hand in, hand out, hang up, leave out, look up, make up, pay back, pick up, put away, put back, put down, put off, put on, put out, shut off, start over, take off, tear down, tear off, tear up, throw away/out, try on, turn down, turn off, turn on, turn up, write down.*

- **Nonseparable two-word verbs:**

    The car **ran into** the light post.

    NOT
    The car ran the light post into.

    Some nonseparable two-word verbs include: *call on, drop in, drop out (of), get along (with), get back (from), get in(to), get off, get on, get out (of), get over, get through (with), grow up, keep on, look out (for), run into, run out (of), watch out (for).*

> **TIP**
>
> Phrasal verbs are generally considered informal. Many times there is a verb with the same meaning that is more formal:
>
> *bring about* = cause
>
> *call off* = cancel
>
> *look over* = review

6. Single-word adjectives come before the nouns they describe. If more than one adjective describes a noun, there is generally a fixed order in which the adjectives appear. A noun usually has no more than a determiner and three adjectives describing it.

Determiner	Number	Opinion	Physical Description	Origin	Material	Noun Modifier	Noun
a		precious	round	South African			diamond
	three		large			hunting	dogs
some		beautiful	green		wooden		chairs

A precious round South African diamond was found in 1952.

Three large hunting dogs ran across the road.

I bought **some beautiful green wooden** chairs.

NOTE: If two or more adjectives fall within the same category, they are separated by a comma. These adjectives can also be reversed or separated by *and* or *or*.

> My art teacher is **creative, well rounded,** *and* **knowledgeable.**

When two or more adjectives fall within separate categories and make sense in only one order, no commas are needed.

> Jocelyn bought **three new wool** sweaters yesterday.

7. Prepositional phrases that modify nouns generally follow the nouns.

> Samuel's work **at the power plant** has dangerous aspects.
>
> NOT
> Samuel's work has dangerous aspects at the power plant.

8. When a prepositional phrase begins a sentence with an intransitive verb (a verb that doesn't take an object), the basic order of the subject and verb must be reversed. This form is usually used to describe a location.

> **On the floor** lie two beautiful Persian carpets.
>
> **In the corner** is an old rocking chair.
>
> **Down the road** strolled two old men.

9. Adjective clauses closely follow the nouns that they describe. (See Chapter 6.)

> The entrance exam **that we took** was very difficult.
>
> NOT
> The entrance exam was very difficult that we took.

10. Adverbs appear at the beginning, middle, and end of sentences depending on the type of adverb used. There are adverbs of time, manner, frequency, and place. Adverbs also comment on what has been said.

   Although the order of adverbs and adverb phrases within a sentence can vary, the following guidelines can be helpful.

- Initial position

Time	**Last night/Yesterday/Two days ago** there was an earthquake in Japan.
Opinion	**Clearly/Honestly/Of course,** the price is too high.
Manner	**Quickly/Happily/Carefully,** we ran across the busy highway.

- Middle position

Frequency	Alana's family **always/never/seldom** goes on a vacation.
	Her family is **often/usually/constantly** at work.
Manner	The teacher **softly/enthusiastically/sadly** announced our grades.

- End position

Place	The children play **outside/in the park/here.**
Time	They begin volunteering **next week/tomorrow/in one month.**
Manner	The doubles team played that ball **well/poorly/badly.**

NOTE: Only two or three adverbials generally appear in one sentence.

Every year, Mr. and Mrs. Santos return by boat to their favorite vacation spot.

Adverbs of time and frequency usually come after those of position and direction.

The children played *in the park* yesterday.

We drive *to school* every Monday.

11. Adverbs should be as close as possible to the verbs, adjectives, adverbs, or clauses that they modify.

> **Mara works diligently in the lab.**
> (Diligently *modifies the verb* works.)
>
> **She is very beautiful.**
> (Very *modifies the adjective* beautiful.)
>
> **We learned sign language surprisingly quickly.**
> (Surprisingly *modifies the adverb* quickly.)
>
> **Amazingly, the plane arrived on time.**
> (Amazingly *modifies the entire* clause.)

12. Adverbs such as *a lot, a little,* and *slightly* limit the word they modify and appear before that word.

> **Ms. Kelly is tired today.**
>
> **Ms. Kelly is a lot more tired today than she was yesterday.**
>
> **Ms. Kelly is a little more tired today than she was yesterday.**
>
> **Ms. Kelly is slightly more tired today than she was yesterday.**

13. When negative adverbs such as *seldom, never, rarely,* and *only once* appear at the beginning of a sentence, *the subject and auxiliary verb are reversed.*

> **Mindy *has* seldom *seen* a better play.**
>
> **Seldom *has* Mindy *seen* a better play.**
>
> **Paloma's mother never *let* her eat dessert.**
>
> **Never *did* Paloma's mother *let* her eat dessert.**

14. The subject pronoun *I* appears at the end of a list of subjects.

> **Linh, Toby, and *I* are roommates.**
>
> **NOT**
> **I, Linh, and Toby are roommates.**

> **TIP**
>
> Make your writing more interesting by varying the types of sentences you write. Start sentences with prepositional phrases or negative adverbs. Use a variety of adverbs that fall at the beginning, middle, or end of a sentence.

SELF CHECK

Correct the errors involving word order.

1. The German new racing cars are winning all the races.

2. The teacher called me on to answer the question.

3. Three weeks ago, I and Norma took the placement test.

4. The hotel needs to know when will you arrive.

5. They hiked last Saturday to the top of the mountain.

> **TIP**
>
> Do not allow friends to edit your papers for you. Ask them to help locate errors in early drafts, but correct the errors yourself. The best and quickest way to become a good writer is to write a lot and to do your own editing.

EDITING PRACTICE

1 *Put a check (✓) next to the sentences that use word order correctly. Correct the sentences that have errors.*

____ 1. Do you know where is the social science building?

____ 2. Nearly every weekend during the winter we go sledding in the mountains.

____ 3. Most passengers get the bus off at the midtown stop.

____ 4. Pierre loves the Cajun spicy shrimp.

____ 5. The woman has a Ph.D. who lives next door.

____ 6. Daniel and Tim are doing their homework over.

____ 7. The professor gave to Jane a book.

____ 8. Where should we meet on Friday night?

____ 9. Les asked me where should we meet on Friday night.

_____10. Pat and Candice in the library are studying math.

_____11. Rarely Mr. Wedner has been on time to an appointment.

_____12. On the table sits a vase of roses.

_____13. Before the last class meeting, I and the professor discussed my course grade.

_____14. John's work involves physics at the university.

2 *Read the following paragraph. Complete the paragraph with the words in the correct order.*

Social values are common ideas or standards that a society has about what is worthwhile, right, and desirable. In countries like Japan, which has a homogeneous population, these values are easy to identify. However, in countries like the United States, with its heterogeneous population, it is _____ to identify the prevailing social
1. slightly more difficult / more slightly difficult
values. People living in countries with _____ may not even be
2. populations mixed / mixed populations
able to identify _____. In other words, when a
3. what their common values are / what are their common values
country has a variety of racial, ethnic, religious, and regional traditions, social values

_____. In the United States, for example, people
4. easily may not be observed / may not be easily observed
living in the North may have different attitudes about time from people in the South. Even though
these core social values _____ to the average person,
5. may not be always obvious / may not always be obvious
they are important bonds that hold a society together.

Naturally, some members of any given society do not always accept all core values.
These individuals are often considered the minority and may be seen as not fitting in.

_____ considered a threat to the stability of society, and the
6. Even they might be / They might even be
society will act to protect the prevailing values. For example, in a society where uniformity is

_____, a value such as individualism will be discouraged. Any
7. a high social priority, / a social high priority
behavior that promotes individualism will be looked on with suspicion.

What can a society do to maintain its core values? Some believe that the values that do not
benefit a society will naturally die out, but others feel that values _____
8. that go against the mainstream
_____. They believe that
culture should be suppressed / should be suppressed that go against the mainstream culture
core values are what _____ and that it is only by
9. hold together a society / hold a society together
_____ that their society will prosper.
10. getting rid of divergent values / getting divergent values rid of

3 *In the following paragraph, the underlined sections have word order errors. Rewrite or move words in each underlined section so that the word order is correct.*

Acupuncture is (1) <u>a Chinese traditional technique</u> of medical treatment. In China, acupuncture has long been used with herbal medicine for pain relief and treatment of (2) <u>other many ailments</u> such as headaches, hay fever, and ulcers. In the West, (3) <u>rarely acupuncture has been used</u> in this way. Acupuncturists have primarily used it as anesthesia and to help patients (4) <u>get pain over</u>; however, its use and popularity are increasing every year. Acupuncture uses a number of very fine metal needles that are inserted into the skin at specific points, depending on the patient's ailment. The needles are twirled and vibrated in specific ways. The depth (5) <u>also of the insertion is</u> important. A battery-powered device was recently developed (6) <u>to deliver to the needles electrical stimulation</u>. (7) <u>Approximately there are</u> 800 acupuncture points that are arranged along fourteen lines running the length of the body from head to foot. These lines, or meridians, are the paths that energy follows throughout the body, and when one of these lines is blocked, illness may result. Many have questioned (8) <u>how does acupuncture work</u>, but are, nevertheless, impressed by its results and (9) <u>eagerly would recommend</u> (10) <u>to others it</u>.

4 *The following paragraph has ten word order errors. Find and correct the errors.*

Young men in many countries of the world must fulfill a military obligation before they are a certain age. Many fully support this requirement while others who live in peaceful countries wonder why is this obligation necessary. It may seem like a burden to impose this on young men for a government. In order to convince new recruits of the positive aspects of military life, the government must convey to the young men the military's importance. However, many young men still attempt to get out of the obligation who don't support the idea of mandatory military requirements. Even though many feel too much time is taken out of their young lives, rarely young men are able to get their obligation out of.

Although there are those who disagree with the mandatory military obligation, completely most citizens still support this so-called "rite of passage." Some support it because they feel secure when their lives and country are protected by citizens who come from all walks of life everyday. Another benefit is military service allows young men to take several years to learn about life and their interests. Most older men remember their few years in the military as a time when they learned about themselves fondly and gained valuable expertise that has helped them in their careers. Some even propose that countries without a military mandatory obligation consider the benefits of this type of program. However, in this day and age, both young men and women must fulfill this obligation if it is going to be fair.

WRITING TOPICS

Choose one of the topics below, and write at least one paragraph. Be sure to use word order carefully. After you complete your first draft, concentrate on editing your work. Keep in mind the editing practice from this chapter.

1. Computers, mobile phones, and faxes are supposed to make our lives easier. Describe the kinds of technology that you use or are familiar with. Where, when, and why do you use these devices? Has this technology made your work easier and your life more convenient? Evaluate the importance of technology in people's lives today.

2. Describe your current living environment. Where do you live? How long have you lived here? Who do you live with? Explain why you like or dislike your living situation.

Go to page 104 for more practice with word order.

CHAPTER 11

Extra Editing Practice

Use the following pieces of writing to practice editing for grammar
points that you have focused on in the previous chapters. When you
edit your own writing, it is important to look for a variety of
grammatical errors; therefore, the exercises in this chapter require that
you edit for more than one type of grammatical structure.

> **TIP**
>
> **Don't forget to schedule editing time into the time you plan
> for writing your essays. Careful editing should take up at least
> ten percent of your writing time. If it takes five hours to write
> an essay, plan to spend at least another thirty minutes
> editing your writing.**

TENSES, MODALS, AND PASSIVE VOICE

1 *Edit carefully for errors in verb tense, modals, and the passive voice. There are __ten__ errors in the following paragraph.*

It is interesting to see how unexpected life events caused people to change and grow. My grandmother is a good example of someone who had unanticipated events change the course of her life and her outlook. She was born during World War I and was raise in a traditional family where the father went to work and the mother had stayed home to take care of the children. She believed that her life will follow the same course. She married early and had three children before the age of twenty-three. Unfortunately, one was died before his first birthday. World War II was the second unexpected event to change the life she had planned for herself. Her husband was send to Europe and killed in France. Before his death, my grandmother had taken evening courses at a local college. She eventually was received her master's degree in social work and worked for the state for thirty years. Because her life didn't follow the path she had planned, she has become a flexible, open-minded person. Unlike many people her age, she accepts modern ideas about marriage, divorce, religion, and pregnancy. She knows from experience that life is unpredictable, and the world will continues to move forward. From her I have learned that we should not have been too rigid or we are disappointed about the paths that our lives take.

TENSES, COORDINATION, AND PARALLEL STRUCTURE

2 *Edit carefully for errors in verb tense, coordination, and parallel structure. There are __ten__ errors in the following paragraph.*

Should I live at home and commute to campus or should I move into the on-campus dormitory? This question runs through the minds of many students as they prepared to enter college. There are definitely benefits to both living situations. Many parents encourage their children to live on campus so the children can experience freedom, friendship, and the responsible of being on their own. Other parents might encourage their children to live on campus so that their children learn to fully appreciate home but all of its comforts. On the other hand, many parents would prefer that their college-age children commute. This option costs less money, keeps children under the parents' control, and students have more time to study and less time to worry about cooking, cleaning, and laundry.

When I made this decision, there were several factors that influence me to live on campus rather than commuting from home. I knew one of the advantages will be meeting other students easily. Other factors that influenced me were the convenience of not having to hunt for a parking space each morning and not having to wake up early only to sit in traffic. However, I have a good friend who lives very close to campus, yet he commutes every day. Not only he has breakfast prepared for him every morning, but he also has a lot of spending money because he isn't paying dorm fees. However, he has made fewer new friends, and he doesn't attend as many parties as I do. Overall, no living situation was perfect. When students make decisions about where they will live the next year, they should realize that there will be both positive and negative aspects to any choice they make.

MODALS, NOUNS, AND DETERMINERS

3 *Edit carefully for errors in the use of modals, nouns, and determiners. There are <u>ten</u> errors in the following paragraph.*

Good communications skills are important, but I believe the most important of these skills is writing well. This skill seems to be necessary in all parts of modern life. With so many informations given in the written form, I find that I judge the other people by the way that they write. Clothing and speech may has conveyed a first impression in the past, but in this day and age, writing may be the only contact we have with other people. I have recently learned the importances of writing in the business world. I have gone on several job interviews and at each one, I was asked to write the short essay. It's clear that employers are looking more and more for the ability to write well. Grammar is obviously important for students. When I was in high school, I didn't realize an importance of grammar and my grades suffered because I shouldn't make myself clearly understood in writing. I learned the hard way about using good grammar and a clear concise writing style. Same lessons can be applied when writing letters, sending email, and jotting down notes to family and friends. Because we may be evaluated by colleagues, peers, family, or friends on our written words, good grammars and writing skills are necessary.

TENSES, PASSIVE VOICE, AND ADJECTIVE CLAUSES

4 *Edit carefully for errors in the use of verb tenses, passive voice, and adjective clauses. There are* <u>ten</u> *errors in the following paragraph.*

In London, England, there are many activities and sights that they are educational as well as fun. Some fun, educational sites included the British Museum, the National Gallery, and the Tower of London. The British Museum, that is one of the busiest tourist attractions in the city, has a vast and diverse collection that may require several days to see. At the National Gallery, some tours are guide to help guests manage the sizable collection. Before it became a busy tourist attraction, the Tower of London has a history that people today finds horrible yet fascinating. Some activities and sights in London that is fun but also educational include wandering around Soho, shopping at a Sunday morning street market, and dining at one of the popular London restaurants. When one was in a foreign country, it's always interesting to watch people have a different culture, language or outlook. Even though these activities are not consider educational in the traditional sense, they teach us lessons that we would not learn if we stayed home.

NOUNS, DETERMINERS, AND WORD ORDER

5 *Edit carefully for errors in the use of nouns, determiners, and word order. There are* <u>ten</u> *errors in the following paragraph.*

The Day of the Dead is the important festival that is celebrated in Mexico and much other Central and South American countries. It is time when people recognize the cycle of life and death. The original celebration was held in July or August during the Aztec month of Miccailhuitontli. In the post-conquest era, Spanish priest moved a holiday to coincide with Christian holiday All Hallows Eve, so now the Day of the Dead is observed on the first two days of November. The day's activities include visiting family gravesites, delivering to these sites flowers and religious amulets, and enjoying a picnic with family and community members. There are very important two points to remember about the Day of the Dead. First, with a complex history it is a holiday, so its observance varies by region and by degree of urbanization. Second, it is not a sad occasion, but rather a time of festivities and joy. Especially, this celebration is important, so even with modern influences, people have kept honoring past generations and will continue to do so for generations to come.

COORDINATION, PARALLEL STRUCTURE, AND CONDITIONALS

6 *Edit carefully for errors in the use of coordination, parallel structure, and conditional sentences. There are <u>ten</u> errors in the following paragraph.*

All Isaac and Juliet can think about is vacation, even though they just graduated from college and started working three months ago. Both of them love their jobs, but they can't believe they won't have a vacation for another nine months. They said that if they had known the company's vacation policy before starting the job, they would negotiate for time off at six months rather than twelve. This will make their first summer without a vacation easier to bear. At this point, all they can do is dream of time off from work. If Isaac takes a vacation now, he would go to some remote location without any distractions from phones, faxes, or receiving email. He would hike, read, relax, and truly appreciate his few days away from work. Juliet, on the other hand, would travel to a place with a lot of people and excitement if she goes on a vacation. She will like to go to a big city with shopping, fine dining and dances. In reality, Isaac nor Juliet has a vacation day in the near future. They tell their friends who are still in school to appreciate the generous amount of time off they have as students, when their friends go on vacation, neither Isaac nor Juliet wants to hear about it! If Isaac and Juliet were back in school, they would have relished each and every day they were not in class. Neither of them realized the importance of vacations until three months ago.

ADVERB CLAUSES AND CONDITIONALS

 Edit carefully for errors in the use of adverb clauses and conditional sentences. There are <u>nine</u> errors in the following paragraph.

According to Michael Korda in his book *Success!*, "success is relative." In other words, what one person considers a success, another may consider a failure. To be successful, each of us has to define the word for ourselves. So that we know when we have achieved our goals. Korda goes on to say that not everyone wants to run a corporation or lead a country, and in fact it may be problematic to start with so grand expectations that are bound to result in failure. In fact, this type of unattainable goal leads to laziness because the goal is so far beyond one's capabilities. Korda suggests that where we make a goal, the goal should be reasonably realistic. After we make a habit of succeeding with moderate goals it's easier to go on to the larger ones. If one had made success a habit, increasing the level of ambition becomes natural and realistic.

Although Michael Korda makes a good point about making success a habit, but I believe it is important to always dream big. If I had listened to his advice earlier, I might not start college. Because no one in my family had ever gone to college before, I didn't think I was capable of college either. However, I had teachers, counselors, and friends who encouraged me. Because their encouragement, I have just finished my second year at a university. If people asked me for advice on achieving success, I would tell them just the opposite of Korda's advice. I will encourage them to define success in grand terms and to make the goals as big as possible.

ADJECTIVE CLAUSES AND NOUN CLAUSES

 Edit carefully for errors in the use of adjective clauses and noun clauses. There are <u>ten</u> errors in the following paragraph.

In many ways, language and dress help define who are we and provide the first impression who people have of us. From language and dress, one may be able to tell the gender, age, and even culture of a total stranger. Language such as "chick" for girl, "dude" for boy, "cool" for good, and "fine" for attractive clearly identifies different generations. Not only does vocabulary distinguish teenagers from their parents, but the intonation or rhythm who their sentences have also places them within a certain age group. Although males and females of the same age may use some of the same vocabulary and intonation, they are likely to choose different words and expressions. Culture also plays a role in the language we use. In Chinese society, it is common to ask if someone has eaten yet. This is a traditional greeting came from a time of poverty and starvation. In many western countries, this greeting would seem strange since the most common greeting in the west is simply to ask how is a person. Similar to language, if we wear also helps identify culture, age, or gender. The socks and shoes, skirt length, or pants style that chooses all give us important information. It is true that is globalization making the world smaller, but the choices are made in language and dress still tell others a lot about us. It has been said that can you tell a book by its cover.

CHAPTER 1 Tenses and Time Shifts

Read the following selection from UCI News. *Choose the correct form of the verb.*

Men, Women Differ in Storing of Emotional Memories

The far-fetched[1] idea that emotionally men are from Mars and women from Venus[2] may have a

biological basis after all. The two sexes _____ different sides of their brains to process
                  1. use / have used

and store long-term memories of emotional experiences, a study shows.

    In testing how men and women store these types of memories, a research team

_____ that the amygdala, an almond-shaped structure on both sides of the brain,
2. finds / found

_____ emotional memories exclusively on the right side of the brain in men and on
3. process / processes

the left side in women.

    "While we don't yet know why this occurs, these results demonstrate a clear gender-

related difference in the formation of emotional memories," said Larry Cahill of the Center for the

Neurobiology[3] of Learning and Memory, who _____ the study. "They also suggest that
                               4. led / will lead

further research on memory must take gender into consideration. . . ."

    In the study, 22 participants—11 women and 11 men—_____ two films,
                               5. viewed / were viewing

one composed of emotionally neutral images and the other of emotionally charged images.

    While the participants _____ the films, the researchers traced brain activity.
                         6. view / viewed

The 11 women revealed significant activity related to memory for the emotional film in the left

amygdala but none in the right one. The 11 men _____ completely opposite results. . . .
                             7. showed / show

    "What's interesting about these tests is the activity is exclusively in the right or

left amygdala and not on the other side," said Cahill, an assistant professor of neurobiology

and behavior.

    "This means that the brains of the men and women in our study could not have been

storing memories of the films in the same way. But we _____ too much more
                            8. don't know / didn't know

than that right now. That's why we must begin to better understand the advantages of sex and

hemisphere differences as the brain stores memories of emotional events."

"Currently these neurobiological results _____ us to go back to the
9. are forcing / were forcing
psychological level to find differences in what men and women remember about emotional events
that previous studies _____."
10. will apparently miss / have apparently missed

[1]**far-fetched** unlikely to be true

[2]**Men are from Mars, Women are from Venus** title of a popular book about the difference in the ways men and women communicate

[3]**neurobiology** the branch of science that deals with the nervous system

CHAPTER 2 Modals

Read the following selection from Omni Magazine. *Choose the correct modal and verb combinations.*

Psychic Pooch

After sustaining a head injury in a 1984 car crash, Victoria Doroshenko suffered from daily, severe epileptic seizures[1]. She often broke bones or injured her head when she fell during these episodes. Then she was frequently confined to a wheelchair. That's when the Washington State woman began searching for a dog that _____ her belongings, pick up her crutches, or
1. can carry / could carry
pull her wheelchair. The dog she found, a golden retriever named Harley, turned out to be more help than Doroshenko _____: Harley, it seems,
2. could ever have imagined / could ever have imagine
_____ when she is about to have a seizure and warns her, sometimes up to 45
3. can sense / can senses
minutes *before* a seizure begins.

Soon after taking Harley home, Doroshenko was startled when the dog suddenly refused to obey commands and began running around her. "I sat down and went into a grand mal",[2] she says. "Ever since, Harley has been forewarning me of seizures. He breaks my falls. If I'm alone, he'll go for help."

How _____ a dog predict epileptic seizures? Reina Berner, executive director of
4. should / could
the New York-based Epilepsy Institute, suggests several possible explanations. Berner says Harley
_____ to detect mild behavioral or physiological changes—imperceptible
5. may have been able / may be able
to humans—that a person _____ before the onset of a seizure. "Or," says Berner,
6. may exhibit / may exhibits
"it _____ that the animal somehow picks up changes in the electromagnetic
7. could have been / could be
fields in the person's brain."

Berner _____ to isolate the cues Harley picks up on so that other dogs

8. would like / could like

_____ as safety companions for people with epilepsy. "Before I got

9. can be trained / may have been trained

my dog," says Doroshenko, "I was afraid and housebound. Harley gave me my life back."

[1]**epileptic seizures** sudden attacks of epilepsy—a medical condition that can make a person become unconscious or unable to control his or her movements for short periods of time

[2]**grand mal** a serious epileptic seizure

CHAPTER 3 Nouns and Determiners

Read the following selection from Alaska Airlines *magazine. Choose the correct determiner and noun form.*

Blue Wonder

Less than half a mile from shore, on _____ small boat in central California's

1. the / a

Monterey Bay, Brenda Peterson had an encounter with nature she'll never forget. "Here we

were, still within sight of land, when we came across a huge superpod of wild dolphins," the

Seattle resident recalls. "We were surrounded by maybe 1,500 of them, leaping clear of

_____ water, again and again, with such speed that _____ bodies never

2. the / a   **3. their / its**

seemed to touch down."

For Peterson and _____ 50 passengers on board, the experience was incredible.

4. other / the other

"There were splashes everywhere," she says. "We were surrounded by a tsunami—a tidal wave[1]

of dolphins."

"It's impossible to observe one of these active, highly intelligent _____ without

5. animals / animal

feeling a sense of respect," agrees Dr. Martin Haulena, staff veterinarian with The Marine Mammal

Center, a nonprofit organization in Sausalito, California. "_____ ocean dwellers evoke[2]

6. Little / Few

such emotional responses from _____ people."

7. the / Ø

And with good reason. Unlike cold-blooded fish, dolphins and porpoises possess what can

best be described as joie de vivre—an undeniable zeal[3] for _____ living. Whether

8. the / Ø

leaping from the water to perform a cartwheel 10 feet in the air, or racing in front of a speeding

pleasure boat to hitch a ride on the vessel's bow wave, these _____ display an obvious

9. animals / animal

delight and an astounding sense of comfort and ease in their buoyant, blue world.

Beginning with Dr. John Lilly's work on _____ dolphin brain, some interesting
                                    10. Ø / the

and even controversial _____ has been done to assess dolphin intelligence, social
                       11. research / researches

behavior, and communication. _____ Scientists have discovered, for example, that when
                             12. Ø / The

wild dolphins gather in large herds they form a definite dominance hierarchy, with individuals

establishing places in the pecking order[4] with the aid of a "signature whistle"—a highly pitched

sound that all other _____ can hear and identify.
                     13. dolphin / dolphins

Some _____ have theorized that these whistles, as well as an array of
     14. researcher / researchers

clicks, clacking noises, and squeaks, may be a form of language (nicknamed dolphinspeak), with

which dolphins can share complex thoughts. _____ people have tried to learn
                                           15. Much / Several

_____ language, attempting to open the doors to future conversations with some of the
16. this / these

most intelligent _____ of our planet.
                 17. cohabitant / cohabitants

"We need not ask what we would gain if we learned to communicate with mammals in

the sea," wrote Captain Jacques Yves Cousteau. "We are a species alone," the French oceanographer

concluded. "Any companionship we find would be a precious reward. . . ."

[1]**tidal wave very large ocean wave**

[2]**evoke produce a strong feeling in someone**

[3]**zeal great interest and eagerness**

[4]**pecking order social order of a group of people or animals**

CHAPTER 4 The Passive Voice

Read the following selection from the New University. *Choose the correct verb.*

Latin American Film Explosion

Several hot Latin American films that are equivalent to Hollywood blockbusters[1]

_____ in a series called the "Festival of Latin American Cinema." In addition
1. will be shown / will be showed

to a wide variety of foreign films, special guest speakers and poetry readings will also be featured

throughout the festival.

The series will present movies that _____ from different parts
                                   2. have collected / have been collected

of Latin America; countries such as Mexico, Chile, and Argentina _____, to
                                                                 3. will be featured / will feature

name a few. According to Jacobo Sefami, associate professor of Spanish and chair of the Department of Spanish and Portuguese, the film festival was created with intentions of providing scholarly perspectives[2] on how different cultures are organized in different places throughout Latin America.

"The idea was to have a diverse type of festival where films _____ from

4. present / are presented

different countries and have different story lines," Sefami said. "Love stories, political stories, and stories with a sense of the diversity of Latin America, not just Mexico, is what

_____ in the program of this series."

5. is being highlighted / is highlighting

According to Sefami, what _____ this year's film festival different than last

6. is made / makes

year's is the fact that more countries _____ in the films. . . .

7. are representing / are being represented

"The idea was to expand on the previous festival, which _____ on

8. had focused / had been focus

Mexico," Sefami said. "This series will feature recent films such as *El Chacotero*, which was very successful in theaters in Chile. I don't know if it will make it to commercial theaters here, but it has the potential to be a blockbuster. These films are not available in commercial theaters here and they are really great films." . . . .

El Chacotero Sentimental [Chile, 1999; Dir. Cristian Galaz; 94 min.] is a film based on a real radio show where anyone can call and tell his or her sentimental[3] problems, while its announcer, Rumpi, tries to guide them with humor. The movie _____ from light

9. is gone / goes

comedy to hard drama to comedy-drama, and it surprisingly succeeds in all three, according to film critics.

The festival _____ as an alternative[4] method to educate students on

10. created / was created

campus. Although the films are in the native language of where the film originates, all of the movies have English subtitles.

Although Sefami said that sometimes people _____ films

11. do not attract to / are not attracted to

with subtitles, he feels that once people try it out and continue to see movies with subtitles, they end up liking these movies.

"Some people are very scared of subtitles. If you go to Mexico and watch movies in a theater, all you hear is English and all you read are Spanish subtitles . . . ," Sefami said. "I think it's

part of education. After one or two movies, you _____ to it. Foreign films are very
12. are get used / get used
important to our own culture, whether it be Japanese films or Middle-Eastern films."

Janine Curiel, a UCI student, commented on how important it is for the university to
be involved in providing a diverse education, "Some students are probably not even aware of
the diversity that exists in their own communities. The festival will be educational and fun at the
same time."

[1]**blockbusters** very successful movies

[2]**perspectives** ways of thinking that are influenced by ones personality, background, or work

[3]**sentimental** love-related (or emotions related to love, sympathy, sadness, etc.)

[4]**alternative** different from what is usual or expected

CHAPTER 5 Coordination and Parallel Structure

Read the following selection from Westways *magazine. Choose the correct forms to ensure coordination and parallel structure.*

Depot of Dreams
A train lover finds beauty and solace at L.A.'s Union Station

Writer and art critic John Ruskin characterized the train station as "the very temple of
discomfort," but he never entered L.A.'s Union Station. Ruskin died in 1900, 39 years before what
is arguably the most beautiful train depot in America was built.

Trains are a metaphor[1] for being transported—by fortune, _____, or
1. romance / romantic
the imagination. Scores of movies have been shot at L.A.'s train depot, including a 1940 William
Holden vehicle titled *Union Station*, in which he plays a railway detective. *Blade Runner, The
Way We Were*, and *Bugsy* were also filmed there. In the Holden movie, you get to see Union
Station newly built. Women loll[2] near the information counter in gloves, hats, and tight,
calf-length skirts. . . .

The station was built to take advantage of L.A.'s year-round blooming season,
_____ arcades link the main waiting areas to patios and courtyards planted with
2. but / so
bougainvillea, birds of paradise, ginger plants, Natal plum. One can sit on the edge of tiled
fountains, contemplate ones fortune, and _____ leaves fall into the water. . . .
3. watch / watches

One of Union Station's most relaxing features, helping the harried[3] traveler to breathe more easily, is its relative quiet. For a contrasting example, think of the constant, brain-jangling din at LAX[4]. The train station's acoustics[5] are so pleasant because its walls are lined with cork, which eliminates echo _____ gives the place a hushed quality. I've been to libraries that
4. yet / and
are noisier than Union Station's waiting areas.

Like the cathedral it resembles, Union Station's two gigantic main rooms are laid out in the shape of a cross. The lobby has 52-foot ceilings, enabling traveler and idler alike to think lofty thoughts, which rise endlessly from their heads and congregate just under the ornate inlaid beamed ceiling. Vermont, Montana, Belgium, _____ all
5. France, Spain, and Tennessee / French, Spanish, and Tennessee
contributed marble for the station's gorgeous floors.

The rich tile work and patterned marble make the waiting rooms appear to be lined with exotic tapestries and rugs. Glass-backed art deco signs list destinations in tiny points of light, hinting that these trains will carry you away to ethereal[6] places. The lobby's brass chandeliers are 10 feet in diameter and weigh 3,000 pounds apiece. They give off the optimistic glow of another era.

It's rare to find such a beautifully appointed place, where you can sit for as long as you like without being eyed suspiciously, without someone coming up and asking if you have a reservation or _____ you to hurry along because the tour bus might leave you behind. This is
6. prompt / prompting
opulence intended not just for the rich _____ designed with everyman in mind, to
7. for / but
sustain and _____ him in his journeys no matter how troubled _____
8. delight / delightful   **9. or / so**
weary he might be—free of charge. Where else does that spirit exist these days? Where else is it as gracefully embodied in our surroundings?

Because it was the last of great passenger terminals to be built on a monumental scale in a major American city _____ no longer gets the kind of peak use it had in its heyday,
10. and / or
Union Station's relative desertedness is poignant now. *I can be patient*, it seems to say. *After all, I am a shrine to purposeful waiting. I know that the values I represent are ageless. The wheels are always turning, and my turn must come around again, soon.*

[1]**metaphor** way of describing something by comparing it to something else

[2]**loll** sit or stand in a relaxed way

[3]**harried** stressed

[4]**LAX** Los Angeles International Airport

[5]**acoustics** the qualities of a room that affect how sound is heard in it

[6]**ethereal** heavenly

CHAPTER 6 Adjectives Clauses

Read the following selection from OC Family Magazine. *Choose the correct form and use of adjective clauses.*

Get on the Piano

Taking piano lessons and solving math puzzles on a computer significantly improve specific math skills of elementary schoolchildren, according to a new study.

The results, which _____ in the March issue of the journal
1. were published / they were published
Neurological Research, are the latest in a series _____ links musical training to the
2. who / that
development of higher brain functions.

Researchers worked with 135 second-grade students at the 95th Street School in Los
Angeles after conducting a pilot study[1] with 102 students. Children _____ were given
3. which / that
four months of piano training as well as time playing with newly designed computer software
scored 27 percent higher on math and fraction tests than other children.

Piano instruction is thought to enhance the brain's "hard wiring"[2] for spatial-temporal
reasoning, or the ability to visualize and transform objects in space and time, says physics
professor Gordon Shaw _____ who led the study.
4. , / Ø
At the same time, the computer game allows children to solve geometric and math puzzles
that _____ their ability to manipulate shapes in their mind.
5. boosts / boost
The findings are significant because a grasp of proportional math and fractions
is a prerequisite to math at higher levels, and children who _____ master these
6. do not / does not
areas of math cannot understand more advanced math that _____ critical[3] to
7. it is / is
high-tech fields.

Students _____ used the software and played the piano also demonstrated a
8. whom / who
heightened ability to think ahead, Shaw says. "They were able to leap ahead several steps on
problems in their heads."

Researchers plan to expand the study to six schools this fall to demonstrate its effectiveness in a variety of settings.

[1] **pilot study** test that is done to see if an idea or product will be successful

[2] **hard wiring** something that is not easily changed

[3] **critical** very important

CHAPTER 7/CHAPTER 8 Adverb Clauses and Conditionals

Read the following selection from the New University. *Choose the correct form and use of adverb clauses and conditionals.*

Feng Shui Rearranges Your Qi

The rebirth of Feng Shui, the ancient Chinese science of architectural design, took the interior design world by storm[1] in the early 1990s and has since become a modern architectural and new age catch phrase[2].

Donna Huhem, a practitioner of non-traditional Feng Shui, fell in love with the ancient science _____ she attended a weekend seminar on the advice of a friend.
1. after / unless

_____ I took the first class, it made sense to me. I understood things about my
2. "When / Where
own house. There was truth to me," Huhem said. . . .

The *New University* invited Huhem into its offices to evaluate the work space and to answer the question "Does the *New U.* have good qi?"[3]

Huhem used the bagua[4] to perform a consultation on the power center of the *New U.*, the office of Editor-in-Chief Shaya Mohajer. . . .

_____ Huhem evaluates a space, she says that she first discusses with the
3. Because / When
client what they feel is going on in their lives as well as what they would like to change about their surroundings.

"Number 1, Feng Shui is about change," Huhem said. "The most common complaint from clients is that something just doesn't feel right about the space or the room."

Huhem asked Mohajer if she felt there _____ challenges to her authority within
4. were / are
the office.

Mohajer pinpointed that she wanted her office space to reflect a stronger position of leadership.

After Huhem and Mohajer verbally consulted, Huhem performed a space clearing using the ganta and dorge. The ganta is a bell that represents the feminine aspect of balance in Feng Shui. The dorge is a small scepter that represents the masculine aspect of balance.

After she did the space clearing, Huhem evaluated Mohajer's office using the bagua, which divides the room into nine imaginary sectors: power, future, relationships, descendents, compassion, self, wisdom, community, and health.

Huhem suggested that Mohajer could strengthen her relationship with the staff if she

_____ her desk out of direct alignment[5] with the door and positioned her chair so there

5. moved / moves

is a wall to support her back.

"There is nothing to block the negative energy if the desk _____ in direct

6. were / is

alignment with the door," Huhem said, noting that during home consultations she also advises clients to move the bed out of direct alignment with an entranceway.

"If your back is exposed, people _____ up on you," Huhem said.

7. could sneak / can sneak

Huhem advised that to maintain a positive flow of qi, Mohajer should get rid of 25 things in her office.

"If you _____ it, get it out," Huhem said. She also advised that Mohajer

8. don't use / didn't use

could further cut unnecessary clutter[6] by giving 25 items that are in good condition to a charity.

According to Huhem clutter is the number one qi-blocker.

"Feng Shui means wind/water and clutter is stagnant; it doesn't allow water to flow," Huhem said.

The water principle of Feng Shui manifests itself in the elements that we can see, such as interiors and room ornamentation. However, the wind principle is more philosophical.

"_____ we can't see the wind, but we can see its effects. We want qi to flow like

9. Although / Ø

a gentle breeze," Huhem said.

Huhem suggested that Mohajer place a fountain in her career sector and move her office couch into the family sector, which would create a more welcoming and open environment in her office.

On a final note, Huhem advised that the *New U.* staff area should also be rearranged to reflect the positive changes that will be made to Mohajer's office space.

The *New U.* editorial staff currently uses desks that are separated by high partitions.

Huhem feels that _____ these desks don't allow colleagues to face one
<u>10. because / even though</u>
another, they don't produce positive energy.

"Cubicles this high tend to isolate people from one another. Personal qi is squished from the sides and blocked from the front," Huhem said. "It's hard to have your vision go beyond the box. It is a bad space for someone who wants to move forward. There is no support from the back."

Huhem promised that once Mohajer and the *New U.* staff implement these spacial changes that the editorial offices will be flowing with positive qi.

[1]**took . . . by storm** become very successful suddenly

[2]**catch phrase** short phrase that is easy to remember and used regularly

[3]**qi** energy in a room (pronounced chee)

[4]**bagua** a grid that sections off a space into nine areas in order to evaluate the space

[5]**alignment** arrangement in a line

[6]**clutter** many things left in a messy way

CHAPTER 9 Nouns Clauses

Read the following selection from the Los Angeles Times. *Choose the correct form and use of noun clauses.*

Excuses Don't Make the Grade

Last week in my senior[1] College Prep English class, as part of a study of eyewitness accounts, I asked the students to read a firsthand description of the Great London Fire. The section was only three pages, and I even gave them two nights to read it.

On the day the reading should have been completed, I asked the students to write a response to _____ , how a witness's account differs from a historical
<u>1. what had they read / what they'd read</u>
one. I always ask anyone who seems unprepared to explain _____ he or she didn't do
<u>2. why / what</u>
the work, rather than faking an answer. Given the length of the assignment plus the amount of time allowed to do it, I figured there wouldn't be many in this category. Boy,[2] was I wrong.

Twenty-five of the 31 students present that day had not so much as opened the book. Their reasons for ignoring the homework were frustrating: "I had baseball practice." "I left class early and didn't know we had anything to do." "I was absent [again] the day you assigned this." "I started to read it, but the phone rang." "The first paragraph was not interesting, so I quit." "I did my math and government homework instead." "I'm not really into reading." And certainly the most honest comment: "I guess I'm just irresponsible."

These responses tell us a lot about why _____

3. are so many capable students / so many capable students are

doing poorly. With the possible exception of working (which may be an economic necessity), all of these excuses involve choices.

When students then fail because of these choices, they still look around for someone to blame. Some get mad at the teacher. "You just grade way too hard," one girl told me accusingly. Some blame it on the class. "I'd be doing good in English if we didn't have to read." And some take it out on long-dead authors. "The problem is that Samuel Pepys is a boring person." After a number of such failures comes the mad scramble to raise low grades before a report card or progress notice goes home. For far too many students, school has turned into a passive "do nothing" affair with occasional bursts of energy and extra credit to stave off[3] a D or worse.

Clearly, school doesn't have to be this way. One need only look at successful students to see a different scenario. Although there are obviously such students at all levels, there tend to be more in the honors classes. However, I have always maintained _____ the difference

4. that / if

between honors students and everyone else has more to do with motivation than brains. Obviously there are some flat-out geniuses in the top track, but the vast majority are there because they have clear goals and know _____ to achieve

5. what do they need to do / what they need to do

them. Period.

This leads to an obvious question: How can we encourage a lot more kids to care about their education? Quite frankly, it's too late for many of my current seniors to somehow redeem

_____ , but is there anything to be done for the masses coming

6. that might have been / what might have been

behind them? The solution has to come from three sources: the teachers, the parents, and the students themselves.

Let's start with teachers. We need to teach _____ significant about our world in
7. where's / what's
order to graduate informed, capable human beings who can think and maneuver their way
through the complexities of life. We should try to present this information in an interesting and
engaging way. We also need to come up with meaningful assessments that are fair and provide
students with an accurate measure of _____.
8. where do they stand / where they stand
Above all, we need to resist "dumbing down"[4] the curriculum. To meet lowered
motivation with lowered standards is tempting. It's both pragmatic and easier, but in the end it
serves no one.

Because a teacher sees a student less than one hour a day, parents obviously still have a
huge role to play. As hard as the task is, they must continue to monitor everything about school
from attendance and homework to behavior and academic schedules. Young people make choices
in high school that will affect the rest of their lives. They need all the adults in their lives, teachers
and parents, to hang in there with them.

Lastly, we come to the key players here. No matter how well _____ or
9. we teach / do we teach
_____, students have to meet us halfway. Caring about
10. how involved parents are / how involved are parents
their education will benefit them in ways they might not even imagine. Skipping homework and
cutting class might sound like carefree alternatives to studying, but academic slacking actually
adds more stress to a student's life. There is increasing pressure from teachers, parents, counselors,
and attendance deans. Poor students often become ineligible to play sports or participate in
certain activities. College and career choices are sharply reduced as mediocre grades stack up. It's a
losing proposition[5] all around.

These years will never return, and it makes me sad to see so many kids coasting through
classes as if their education were a joke. High schools are not perfect institutions, but they have
the potential to provide critical knowledge. For many students, their U.S. history class may be the
last time they ever encounter the fascinating process by which this country came to be. Senior
English may offer their only exposure to Shakespeare.

We fought long and hard to get kids out of the labor force and into schools in an attempt
to guarantee a universal standard of education for everyone, regardless of social class. When I

encounter bored, unprepared students, I wonder if any of them realize _____ preferable

11. that / how

school is to working in a coal mine or textile factory. But they probably didn't read that chapter on

the Industrial Revolution.

[1] **senior** last year of high school

[2] **Boy** word said to emphasize a statement

[3] **stave off** stop something from affecting you

[4] **dumbing down** make easier

[5] **losing proposition** bad plan

CHAPTER 10 Word Order

Read the following selection from The Washington Post. *Choose the correct word order.*

A First Class Party

It was easy to give postman Michael Wilson a surprise party. Easy because when Barbara

Abramowitz asked Wilson if he could bring _____ at about 2

1. the mail to her house / to her house the mail

P.M. one day last week, she knew he'd be there.

He's there when it snows, leaving the mail on the back porch so elderly residents won't

slip on the ice. He's there bringing _____ if no one's

2. to the door the newspaper / the newspaper to the door

home, or retrieving the _____ can from the curb on trash day. Carrying

3. garbage empty / empty garbage

irradiated[1] mail, wearing _____ gloves, on or off antibiotics, he's there, still

4. white rubber / rubber white

smiling, still part of the life of this neighborhood in Northwest Washington.

He is a constant. A sure thing in an uncertain time. And these days, that turns folks into

heroes. Even if it is just the neighborhood variety. "We live in a big city," says Abramowitz, "but he

makes our neighborhood like living in a small town." And residents wanted to say thanks for that.

It's just after 2 and when Wilson knocks, about a half-dozen people crowd the door.

Lillian Kronstadt is there. She's made her special three-layer Jell-O mold, and her 4-year-old

grandson, Max, who _____ to the door to greet Wilson on his rounds, yells

5. always runs /runs always

"Surprise!" and hugs his legs.

Wilson, 35, is speechless for a few seconds, then says, "You did this for me?"

For a moment it seems the letter carrier might tear up. But he is quickly assaulted by well-wishes and neighbors and their sweets, and his tears retreat.

Wilson knows _____ of the past seven
    6. along his route the folks / the folks along his route
years, but he didn't know a party was brewing. Abramowitz hatched the idea[2], then called some neighbors and followed Wilson along his route a few days ago, slipping invitations into mailboxes.

"I think since September 11, there's been a lot more awareness that we need to thank people for what they do," says Abigail Wiebenson, director of the nearby Lowell School, which always gets tons of mail. "Especially if they're small things, because those are the people we tend to take for granted[3]."

Wilson, who lives in suburban Clinton, Maryland, with his wife and two daughters, doesn't do big, dramatic, save-the-day kinds of feats, residents say. But they count on him for knowing the names of kids and grandkids and playmates and pets, for keeping track of the minutiae[4] and mail along his 167 stops.

Along with the cake and soft drinks were quite a few presents: cards with a little something tucked inside, and one rather unorthodox gift…

Wilson protests the cake, _____
    7. which says in red cursive script, "Michael Wilson is the best" / "Michael
_____
is the best," which says in red cursive script
"I don't know the right things to say," he says. "I _____ people the same way
    8. just treat / treat just
I want to be treated."

When people say "I appreciate _____," that makes the job special,
    9. what do you do / what you do
he says. Like when residents invite him into their lives. "They'll say 'My daughter is going to graduate, do you want to come by?' . . . There are so many professionals up here, they could

_____ their noses up[5], but they don't do that at all."
10. really turn / turn really
Henrietta Schulman, 78, sits near Wilson. After her husband died last year she moved from her house of 57 years to a _____ community, but she came
    11. suburban retirement / retirement suburban
back "to see Michael." "He's special," Schulman says. "I called and told the post office they should have more like him."

It's a little after 3 and the party is winding down. People have to return to their jobs and appointments and routines. And Wilson returns to his mail truck, loaded down with cake and gifts and the gratitude of the people he sees every day.

[1] **irradiated** treated with x-rays to eliminate poisonous substances

[2] **hatched the idea** thought of the idea

[3] **to take for granted** to underestimate the value of something or someone

[4] **minutiae** very small, unimportant details

[5] **turn their noses up** to see or regard someone or something as inferior

APPENDIX 2 Irregular Verbs

Base Form	Simple Past	Past Participle	Base Form	Simple Past	Past Participle
be	was, were	been	meet	met	met
beat	beat	beaten/beat	pay	paid	paid
become	became	become	put	put	put
begin	began	begun	quit	quit	quit
bend	bent	bent	read	read	read
bet	bet	bet	rid	rid	rid
bind	bound	bound	ride	rode	ridden
bite	bit	bitten	ring	rang	rung
bleed	bled	bled	rise	rose	risen
blow	blew	blown	run	ran	run
break	broke	broken	say	said	said
bring	brought	brought	see	saw	seen
build	built	built	seek	sought	sought
buy	bought	bought	sell	sold	sold
catch	caught	caught	send	sent	sent
choose	chose	chosen	set	set	set
come	came	come	shake	shook	shaken
cost	cost	cost	shine	shone/shined	shone/shined
creep	crept	crept	shoot	shot	shot
cut	cut	cut	show	showed	shown
deal	dealt	dealt	shrink	shrank/shrunk	shrunk/shrunken
dig	dug	dug	shut	shut	shut
do	did	done	sing	sang	sung
draw	drew	drawn	sit	sat	sat
eat	ate	eaten	sleep	slept	slept
fall	fell	fallen	slide	slid	slid
feed	fed	fed	speak	spoke	spoken
feel	felt	felt	speed	sped/speeded	sped/speeded
fight	fought	fought	spend	spent	spent
find	found	found	spin	spun	spun
fit	fit	fit	spit	spit/spat	spat
flee	fled	fled	split	split	split
fly	flew	flown	spread	spread	spread
forbid	forbade	forbidden	spring	sprang	sprung
forecast	forecast	forecast	stand	stood	stood
forget	forgot	forgotten	steal	stole	stolen
forgive	forgave	forgiven	stick	stuck	stuck
freeze	froze	frozen	sting	stung	stung
get	got	gotten	stink	stank/stunk	stunk
give	gave	given	strike	struck	struck/stricken
go	went	gone	string	strung	strung
grind	ground	ground	swear	swore	sworn
grow	grew	grown	sweep	swept	swept
hang	hung	hung	swim	swam	swum
have	had	had	swing	swung	swung
hear	heard	heard	take	took	taken
hide	hid	hidden	teach	taught	taught
hit	hit	hit	tear	tore	torn
hold	held	held	tell	told	told
hurt	hurt	hurt	think	thought	thought
keep	kept	kept	throw	threw	thrown
know	knew	known	understand	understood	understood
lay	laid	laid	undertake	undertook	undertaken
lead	led	led	upset	upset	upset
leave	left	left	wake	woke	woken
lend	lent	lent	wear	wore	worn
let	let	let	weave	wove	woven
lie	lay	lain	weep	wept	wept
light	lit/lighted	lit/lighted	win	won	won
lose	lost	lost	wind	wound	wound
make	made	made	withdraw	withdrew	withdrawn
mean	meant	meant	write	wrote	written

Subject-verb agreement means that a verb must agree with its subject. It must agree in person and in number. Here are some examples of subject-verb agreement listed by verb tense.

SIMPLE PRESENT

Singular		Plural	
I	work.	We	work.
You	work.	You	work.
He/She/It	works.	They	work.

SIMPLE PAST

Singular		Plural	
I	worked.	We	worked.
You	worked.	You	worked.
He/She/It	worked.	They	worked.

PRESENT PROGRESSIVE

Singular		Plural	
I	am working.	We	are working.
You	are working.	You	are working.
He/She/It	is working.	They	are working.

PAST PROGRESSIVE

Singular		Plural	
I	was working.	We	were working.
You	were working.	You	were working.
He/She/It	was working.	They	were working.

PRESENT PERFECT

Singular		Plural	
I	have worked.	We	have worked.
You	have worked.	You	have worked.
He/She/It	has worked.	They	have worked.

PAST PERFECT

Singular		Plural	
I	had worked before.	We	had worked before.
You	had worked before.	You	had worked before.
He/She/It	had worked before	They	had worked before.

SUBJECT-VERB AGREEMENT RULES

1. There can only be one –s ending. It is either on the subject or on the verb.

   An advertisement help**s** sell products to the public.
   Advertisement**s** help sell products to the public.

2. In the simple present tense, add an –s ending to most verbs that follow third person singular subjects.

   ***Billy's uncle* lives** near the fire station.
   In many cultures, ***one* leaves** home for the first time at marriage.
   ***The university* is** on the corner of Campus Drive and Mesa Avenue.

3. A subject and verb must agree even when separated by a clause or phrase.

   The language problem that we encountered when we were on vacation **happens** to most people who visit foreign countries.

4. The correlative conjunctions *both . . . and, either . . . or,* and *neither . . . nor* follow subject-verb agreement rules.

   • Use the plural verb with *both . . . and.*

   Both buying real estate **and** investing in the stock market **are** good long-term investment strategies.

   • The closest noun and verb must agree with *either . . . or* and *neither . . . nor.*

   Either the hospital or ***pharmacies* supply** the medicine she needs. / Either pharmacies or the ***hospital* supplies** the medicine she needs.
   Neither the lotion nor special ***creams* erase** the signs of aging. / Neither special creams nor the ***lotion* erases** the signs of aging.

APPENDIX 4 | Punctuation

This appendix gives you punctuation rules, which can assist you in editing for correct punctuation. Keep this list handy so that you can refer to it when writing.

PERIODS, QUESTION MARKS, AND EXCLAMATION POINTS

1. Use a period to end a sentence.

    There is a test next Monday.

2. Use a question mark to end a direct question.

    Do we have to study?

3. Use an exclamation point to end a sentence that expresses surprise, excitement, or anger.

    It's that soon!

COMMA

1. Use a comma to separate words, phrases, or clauses in a series.

    We brought sandwiches, juice, and cookies to the party.

2. Use a comma to separate independent clauses joined by a coordinating conjunction.

    It is a beautiful day for swimming, *but* the pool is closed.

3. Use a comma after introducing an adverbial phrase or clause.

    On the last day of school, students and teachers usually celebrate.

    Although the price of gasoline is going up, people are still traveling by car.

4. Use a comma with nonrestrictive adjective clauses.

    Valentine's Day, which is celebrated on February 14, is a very busy day for florists.

SEMICOLON

1. Use a semicolon to link closely related independent clauses.

    The election is tomorrow; the polls open at 7:00 A.M.

2. Use a semicolon or period before the transitions *however, nevertheless, nonetheless, therefore, moreover, furthermore, otherwise, thus.* Notice that commas are used after transitions.

    Julia will graduate in a few months; therefore, she has started to look for a job in her field.

    Julia will graduate in a few months. Therefore, she has started to look for a job in her field.

COLON

Use a colon to introduce a series of examples after an independent clause.

    The salad had three ingredients: tomatoes, cucumbers, and lettuce.

CAPITALIZATION

1. Capitalize proper nouns.

Names of people and their titles	John Smith, Dr. Joan Chavez, Aunt Dorothy, Professor Yi
Names of places and things	the Eiffel Tower, the University of New Mexico, the Golden Gate Bridge
Names of countries	Canada, the Philippines, Indonesia, Nepal
Names of languages	French, Spanish, Hebrew, English
Names of nationalities	German, American, Indian, Costa Rican
Names of religions	Buddhism, Catholicism, Judaism, Islam
Names of academic courses	Biology 101, Humanities 200A
Directional names	the East Coast, the Deep South, the North Pole, Southern Florida

2. Capitalize proper adjectives.

Names of nationalities	French crepes, Mexican restaurant, Chinese artifact
Names of religions	Jewish nation, Christian people, Buddhist monk
Names of brands	Apple computer, Nike running shoes, Bayer aspirin

3. Do not capitalize:

Names of seasons	summer, winter, spring, fall/autumn
Articles, prepositions	the United States, the Department of Chemistry
After a semicolon	My brother is a baseball fanatic; he goes to every home game.

UNDERLINE OR ITALICIZE

Titles of books	The Great Gatsby, *Eye on Editing*, The Perfect Storm
Titles of magazines	*Sports Illustrated*, Time, *People*
Titles of newspapers	The New York Times, *The Wall Street Journal*
Titles of movies and plays	*E.T.*, African Queen, *A Chorus Line*, Cats

QUOTATION MARKS

Titles of short stories	"The Legacy," "The Twenty-seventh Man"
Titles of articles in a newspaper or magazine	"Economic Outlook Looks Bright," "Get on the Piano"
Titles of poems	"Beautiful Old Age," "Birches"

APPENDIX 5 Prepositions

A preposition connects a noun or a pronoun to the rest of a sentence and indicates a relationship, for example of time, place, or position.

Prepositions are usually one word but can also be two or more words. The most frequently used one-word prepositions are *at, by, for, from, in, of, on, to,* and *with.* Some prepositions with more than one word are *according to, along with, away from,* and *in front of.*

Many prepositions are frequently combined with adjectives and verbs. Some adjective and verb combinations are *bad at* and *interested in.* Some verb and preposition combinations are *believe in* and *belong to.*

This appendix gives you preposition guidelines that can assist you in editing for the correct use of prepositions in your writing. There are also two lists of frequently used adjective-preposition combinations and verb-preposition combinations. Keep these lists and guidelines handy so that you can refer to them when writing.

TYPES OF PREPOSITIONS

Here are some common prepositions, listed by the type of relationship they indicate:

1. Prepositions of time

month/year	*in*	Aidan arrived *in* June. He arrived *in* 1999.
day/date	*on*	He began classes *on* Monday. He began classes *on* June 5.
specific time	*at*	The class started *at* 9:00 A.M.
general time	*in*	The classes ended *in* the evening/afternoon/morning.
approximate time	*about*	I'll be home *about* 2:00.
	around	Let's meet *around* 5:00.
	between	He said he'll call *between* 9 and 10 o'clock.
duration	*for*	My family lived in Guam *for* six years.
	through	I have thought of you often *through* the past years.

2. Prepositions of place

city/country	*in*	Fred lived *in* Toronto for three years. He lived *in* Canada for five years.
street	*on*	He worked *on* Battery Street.
address	*at*	He lives *at* 16 Queen Lane.
motion	*to*	He goes *to* the park for lunch. (*walk to, run to, drive to, ride to, race to, fly to*)
	toward	They walked *toward* me.

3. Prepositions of position

on	The book is *on* the desk.
in	The lecture notes are *in* my notebook.
at	Let's meet *at* the library.
beside	The dog is sitting *beside* its owner.
between	My house is *between* the library and the bridge.

Some other prepositions that commonly show position are: *above, across, against, along, among, before, behind, below, beneath, beside, between, beyond, by, down, inside, into, near, outside, over, past, under, up.*

4. Prepositions of reason

for	They will do the job *for* minimum wage.
by	He was pleased *by* her kind words.
about	We are concerned *about* the news.

5. Prepositions of manner

by	He can understand their accent *by* listening carefully.
at	She is good *at* speaking foreign languages.
with	They finished the test *with* ease.

6. Preposition of comparison

like	We are so close that he is *like* my brother.
as	We play tennis only *as* amateurs.

7. Preposition of possession

of	Dino is a good friend *of* mine.

ADJECTIVE + PREPOSITION COMBINATIONS

This list contains some common adjective + preposition combinations. Check an ESL or learner's dictionary under the adjective for any adjective + preposition combinations that are not on this list.

A accustomed to
afraid of
amazed at/by
angry at
anxious about
ashamed of
aware of
awful at

B bad at
bored with/by

C capable of
concerned about
content with
curious about

D dependent on
different from

E eager for
envious of
excited about

F familiar with
fond of

friendly to
full of
famous for

G glad about
good at
guilty of

H happy about
homesick for

I inferior to
interested in

J jealous of

K known for

L limited to
lucky at

M mad at/about

N nervous about

O opposed to

P pleased about
proud of

R ready for
responsible for

S sad about
safe from
satisfied with
sick of
similiar to
slow at
sorry for/about
suitable for
superior to
surprised about/at/by

T tired of
terrible at

U upset with

W worried about

VERB + PREPOSITION COMBINATIONS

This list contains common verb + preposition combinations. Check an ESL dictionary under the verb for any verb + preposition combinations that you cannot find on this list.

A accuse s.o. of s.t.
adapt to
admit to
advise against
agree with s.o. about s.t.
apologize for
apply to/for
approve of
argue with s.o. about s.t.
arrive at

B believe in
belong to
blame s.o. for s.t.

C care about/for
choose between
combine s.t. with
come from
compare s.o./s.t. to/with
complain to s.o. about s.t.
concentrate on
consist of
contribute to
cooperate with
count on

D deal with
decide on
depend on
disapprove of
dream about/of

E escape from
excel at
excuse s.o. for

F feel like
fight for
forget about
forgive s.o. for

G glance at
gossip about
graduate from

H happen to
hear about/of s.t.
hear from s.o.
hide from
hope for

I insist on
intend to
interfere with
introduce s.o. to s.o.
invite s.o. to s.t.

K know about

L listen to
look at
look for
look forward to
learn from
live on

M matter to

O object to

P participate in
pay for
plan on

prepare for
prevent s.o./s.t. from
profit from
protect s.o./s.t. from
prohibit s.o. from

R read about
recover from
rely on
rescue from
respond to

S search for
speak to/with s.o. about s.t.
stare at
stop from
subscribe to
substitute for
succeed in

T take advantage of
take care of
talk to/with s.o. about s.t.
thank s.o. for s.t.
think about/of

V vote for

W wait for
worry about

APPENDIX 6 Phrasal Verbs

A Phrasal verb is a combination of a verb and one or two particles. Particles and prepositions look the same, but particles change the meaning of the verb. Phrasal verbs are commonly used in informal speech; there is usually a more formal verb that has the same meaning. For example, *select* is considered more formal than *pick out*. The following is a list of some commonly used phrasal verbs. Use this list as a reference while writing.

A ask out — ask s.o. for a date

B break up — end a relationship
bring up — raise children / introduce a topic

C call back — return a phone call
call off — cancel
call on — visit s.o. / ask a student to speak in a class
call up — call on the telephone
catch on — understand / become popular
catch up with — reach the same level
check in — register at a hotel
check into — investigate
check out — borrow a book from the library / investigate
check out of — leave a hotel
check up on — make sure s.t. is done correctly by s.o.
cheer up — make someone feel better
clean up — make clean
come across — meet s.o. without prior arrangement / find s.t. accidentally
come out — become known
cross out — draw a line through
cut out — stop an irritating activity

D do over — repeat
drop by — visit without an invitation
drop off — take s.o. or s.t. someplace

drop out of — to stop going to school or an activity

F figure out — understand (after thinking about)
fill out — complete a form or questionnaire
fill up — fill completely
find out — discover information

G get along with — be friendly with s.o.
get back from — return
get in — enter a car / arrive in a place
get off — leave an airplane, bicycle, bus, subway, train
get on — enter an airplane, bicycle, bus, subway, train
get out of — leave a car / avoid work or an unpleasant activity
get over — become well after a sickness
get through — finish
get up — rise from a bed or chair
give back — return s.t. to its owner
give in — agree after disagreement
give up — stop trying
go out — leave home for entertainment
go over — review
grow up — become an adult

H	hand in	give an assignment to teacher or supervisor
	hand out	distribute
	hang out	spend time in a particular way / spend time with particular people
	hang up	finish a telephone call / put clothes on a hanger
	have on	wear clothing
	help out	assist
K	keep on	continue
	keep out of	not enter / not allow s.o. to enter
	keep up with	go as fast as
	kick out	force s.o. to leave
L	leave out	do not include
	look after	take care of
	look into	investigate
	look over	review carefully
	look up	try to find in a book or on the Internet
M	make up	invent / complete late work
N	name after/for	give a baby someone else's name
P	pass away	die
	pass out	faint / distribute
	pick out	select
	pick up	go to get someone in a car / take s.t. into one's hand
	point out	call attention to
	put away	put s.t. in its proper place
	put back	return s.t. to its original place
	put off	postpone
	put on	put clothes on
	put out	extinguish a cigarette or fire
	put up with	tolerate

Q	quiet down	become quiet
R	run into/across	meet without prior arrangement
	run out of	finish the supply of s.t.
S	show off	behave boastfully
	show up	appear
	shut off	stop a machine, light, faucet
	shut up	stop talking
	speak up	talk louder / give an opinion
	stay up	remain awake
T	take after	resemble
	take off	remove clothing / leave on a trip
	take out	remove s.t. / take s.o. on a date
	take over	take control
	take up	begin a new activity
	tear down	demolish
	tear up	rip into small pieces
	think over	consider carefully
	throw away/out	get rid of
	throw up	vomit
	try on	put clothing on to see if it fits
	try out	audition / test
	turn down	decrease volume / reject an offer
	turn in	go to bed / submit an assignment
	turn off	stop a machine, light, faucet
	turn on	start a machine, put on a light or faucet
	turn out	extinguish a light
	turn up	increase (volume)
U	use up	use completely
W	wake up	stop sleeping
	watch out	be careful
	wear out	become weak or useless

APPENDIX 7 Problem Words and Phrases

This list contains some commonly misused words and phrases. As you come across other words and phrases that are problems for you, add them to this list.

- **Advice (noncount noun) / advise (verb)**

  She gave me some good *advice*.

  I *advised* him not to drop the class.

- **Affect (verb) / effect (count noun)**

  Jim's worries *affected* his work.

  Jim's worries had a negative *effect* on his work.

- **Agree on + something / agree with + someone**

  We *agreed on* all the answers.

  She *agrees with* her father.

- **All of *a* sudden**

  All of a sudden the energy went out.
  NOT
  All of the sudden . . .

- **As *a* result**

  I passed the test. *As a result,* I can get my license.
  NOT
  As the result . . .

- **Because (+ clause) / because of (+ noun)**

  Because she had an appointment, she couldn't leave early.

  Because of the appointment, she couldn't leave early.

- **Belief (count noun) / believe (verb)**

  They have strong *beliefs*.

  They *believe* in truth and justice.

- **Beside (next to) / besides (in addition to)**

  He sat *beside* me at the ceremony.

  Besides working together, we also take a class in the evening.

- **Had better**

  You *had better* see a doctor.

  You*'d better* see a doctor.
  NOT
  You better . . .

- **Care about (to be interested in) / care for (to take care of)**

  I don't *care about* my grades.

  I have to *care for* my grandmother.
  NOT
  I have to care about her.

- **Concern / to be concerned about**

  Environmental problems *concern* me.

  I *am concerned about* environmental problems.

- **Day after day**

  We study *day after day* to improve our knowledge.
  NOT
  . . . days after days . . .

- **Despite**

  Despite her effort, she couldn't pass the exam.
  NOT
  Despite of her effort . . .

- **Different from**

  I am different *from* my friends.
  NOT
  . . . different than . . .

- **Each / every + singular noun**

  Each child has a toy.

  Every mother loves her children.

- **Emphasize / put emphasis on**

  The instructor *emphasized* the importance of grammar.

  She *put a lot of emphasis on* verbs.
  NOT
  The instructor emphasized on grammar.

- **Even (adverb/intensifer)**

  He doesn't *even* know his father.
  NOT
  He even doesn't . . .

- **Exist**

    Those problems *exist* everywhere.
    NOT
    . . . are exist . . .

- **Face / to be faced with**

    We *face* new issues every day.
    We *are faced with* new issues every day.

- **Hope**

    I *hoped* you would come.
    I *hope* you can come. I *hope* you will come.
    NOT
    I hope I would come.

- **In other words**

    It's broken. *In other words,* it doesn't work.
    NOT
    In another word . . .

- **In spite of**

    In spite of her diet, she couldn't lose
        weight.
    NOT
    In spite her diet . . .

- **In the first place**

    In the first place, you shouldn't be here.
    NOT
    In a first place . . .

- **Know / meet**

    I *met* him in high school.
    I *have known* him since then.
    Note: Use MEET not KNOW when talking
    about first getting to know someone.

- **Matter / it doesn't matter if**

    It doesn't matter if they are late.
    NOT
    It doesn't matter they are late.

- **Most / most of the**

    Most children obey their parents.
    Most of the children obey their parents.
    NOT
    Most of children . . .

- **Nowdays**

    Nowadays, most people have computers.
    NOT
    Now a days . . .

- **On campus**

    We want to live *on campus.*
    NOT
    . . . in campus.

- **One of the (+ plural noun)**

    One of the men has a new car.
    NOT
    One of the man . . .

- **People**

    The *people* are living in poverty.
    NOT
    The people is . . .

- **Would rather**

    He *would rather* be in China.
    He*'d rather* be in China.
    NOT
    He rather . . .

- **Succeed (verb) / success (noun) /
  successful (adjective)**

    We *succeed* because we value *success* and
        we want to be *successful.*

- **Than (conjunction with comparatives) /
  then (adverb - *at that time*)**

    I am taller now *than* I was *then.*

- ***The* United States**

    We live in *the United States* now.
    NOT
    . . . in United States

- **Wish (for things that are not real/true) -
  Hope (for things that are possible)**

    She *wishes* she had a pet.
    She *hopes* she gets one soon.
    NOT
    She wishes she has . . .

- **Year-old / years old**

    He is a *ten-year-old* boy.
    He is *ten years old.*

APPENDIX 8 Using Quotations

Many writers use quotations to strengthen their argument. Quotations are exact words from a print or nonprint source. Be sure to use the exact spelling and punctuation from the original source.

FORMING SENTENCES WITH QUOTATIONS

1. Introduce a quotation with its source (the writer/speaker's name or article/book's title) and a signal verb such as *say* or *write*. The source may be given at the beginning, middle, or end of your sentence. Punctuation is important when using quotations; notice where commas, periods, and quotation marks occur in the following example.

    Franklin Delano Roosevelt said, "We have nothing to fear but fear itself."

    "We have nothing to fear but fear itself," said Franklin Delano Roosevelt.

    "We have nothing to fear," said Franklin Delano Roosevelt, "but fear itself."

2. Quotations may also be introduced with a signal phrase such as *according to,* or an introductory clause. Notice where commas, periods, and quotation marks occur.

    According to Dr. Beth Besch, "Children don't understand that their words can harm others, so they must be taught that words can hurt just like hitting or pushing."

    Dr. Beth Besch discusses teaching children the significance their words have: "Children don't understand that their words can harm others, so they must be taught that words can hurt just like hitting or pushing."

3. The signal verbs that introduce quotations are generally in the simple present or the simple past tense. If the quoted material comes from the past, the signal verb is usually in the past. If the quoted material comes from the present, the signal verb is usually in the present. However, there are exceptions to these guidelines.

In *Writing from A to Z* the authors **contend,** "Editing and revising **should be done** in separate readings of the manuscript, because revising **focuses** on the larger elements of content and organization, and editing **focuses** on sentences and words."

(The quotation states a widely held belief and is in the present tense, so the signal verb contend *is in the simple present.)*

Studies on smoking **found,** "when heavy smokers **decreased** their smoking by half for two or three months, levels of certain tobacco-related toxins in their bodies **did not go down.**"

(The results discussed in the quotation were found in the past and the quotation is in the past, so the signal verb found *is in the simple past.)*

In 1965 Martin Luther King, Jr. **said,** "I **have** a dream that one day this nation **will rise up** and **live** out the true meaning of its creed."

(The signal verb said *is in the past because the quotation is from the past even though the quoted material is in the present and future.)*

FORMING SENTENCES WITH BLENDED QUOTATIONS

1. It is not always necessary to use a full sentence from the original source as the examples above have done. Many times it is preferable to use only part of the original sentence and blend it into your own sentence.

    In <u>The Resourceful Writer</u>, William Barnwell and Robert Dees suggest using "quotations to support or further explain your points, but do not depend on them too heavily."

Writing is used to express your point of view on a particular topic; however, academic writing relies on "balancing your voice with the ideas, research, and theories of other people," according to Holten and Marasco.

Note: When quoted material is shortened, the author's original meaning must not be changed in any way.

2. Use brackets [ ] to grammatically blend quoted material into your own sentences. Brackets are also used to clarify unclear references in quoted material.

When Mrs. Mallard is told the news of her husband's death, "she [weeps] at once, with wild abandonment," as she thinks of the freedom she now has.

As Gilbert Clandon goes through his deceased wife's belongings, he sees that "she had left it [her diary] to him, as her legacy."

USING SENTENCES WITH QUOTATIONS

1. Always give an explanation of the quoted material's significance. Do not simply drop a quotation between your own sentences and expect the reader to understand it.

The Juvenile Justice System was developed on the belief that children who have committed crimes still have the potential to "be developed into productive citizens instead of adult criminals," and it is the responsibility of American society to provide the necessary help to these at-risk children.

NOT

The Juvenile Justice System was developed on the belief that children who have committed crimes can still be helped. "At-risk children must be developed into productive citizens instead of adult criminals." It is the responsibility of American

society to provide the necessary help to these at-risk children.

Tip: Plagiarism is taking personal credit for another person's words or ideas by not referring to this person and not using quotation marks. The rules for plagiarism are different in each country. Consult your instructor or any book on the research process to make sure that you are following the guidelines for avoiding plagiarism.

2. The first time an authority is quoted, give his or her full name and other available information related to the quotation such as book or article title, year of publication, or page number. The next time the same authority is cited, only the last name is given. If another reference is close by, a pronoun is used.

"The Kansas City School District is a very upsetting situation," said Larry Orbach, a Washington University sociologist who has studied the district for years.

To Orbach, the lesson from Kansas City is clear: Money can't buy good schools.

He says this is especially obvious in "urban districts where poverty leaves many children ill-equipped to learn."

Tip: Stating the source of a quotation strengthens the writer's ideas in the readers' eyes and gives them the opportunity to refer to the writer's original sources.

3. Signal verbs that introduce quotations have a meaning. Be sure to use the correct verb for the meaning you want to convey.

- To introduce most quotations use: *add, analyze, announce, consider, describe, discuss, explain, express, illustrate, inform, mention, note, notify, observe, point to, present, recognize, remark, report, say, state, suggest, tell, write*

  The paper reported that the FBI is analyzing "evidence that was obtained at the crime scene."

- To introduce quotations that provide additional information use: *add, continue, further discuss, further explain, further illustrate, further state, later express, later mention,* or *later observe.*

> The president further illustrated his belief in government subsidized childcare by "increasing funding by 15% in the coming year."

- To introduce quotations that present opinions use: *acknowledge, advise, argue, agree, assert, believe, caution, charge, claim, contend, criticize, declare, demand, deny, disagree, emphasize, hold, indicate, imply, maintain, object, oppose, propose, support, think, urge, warn*

> In Dean Schulberg's editorial, he contends that "grade inflation must come to an end if a university degree is to mean anything."

- To introduce quotations that are questions or question an established belief use: *ask, inquire, question, wonder.*

> At the end of his presentation, Professor Jeffries wondered whether or not parents today have "the knowledge of how to discipline their children" when they received little discipline themselves as youngsters.

- To introduce quotations that respond use: *agree, answer, concur, disagree, dispute, reply, respond.*

> The committee concurs with earlier findings that "welfare programs only work in a limited number of cases."

- To introduce quotations that conclude use: *conclude* or *realize.*

> The paper concludes with a plea for "further research to fully answer the questions we still have regarding the need for a space program."

Sometimes you will include the title of a piece of writing that a quotation comes from. Underline or *italicize* the titles of books, magazines, and newspapers and put quotation marks around the titles of articles and short stories.

THREE QUICK STEPS TO USING QUOTED MATERIAL

1. Introduce the quotation with the author's name and give the quotation. Do not simply drop the quotation into your paper without giving credit to the original source.

2. Blend the quoted material into your own sentence whenever possible.

3. Add an additional sentence that explains or clarifies the quotation. Do not expect your readers to understand the importance of the quotation. It is your responsibility to explain it.

WRITING TOPICS / PRACTICE WITH QUOTED MATERIAL

Choose one of the topics below, and write at least one paragraph. Be sure to use quotations. After you complete your first draft, concentrate on editing your work. Keep in mind the guidelines for using quoted material from this appendix.

1. Select an interesting article or book that you have recently read. Either explain the author's point of view or describe one character from the reading. Use at least two quotations to support your comments.

2. Conduct an interview of two to three people about whom they believe is the most important public figure in the world today. Go on to find out why they have chosen this person. You may choose to ask them about public figures from the past too. Report the results of your interview, and use several quotations from the interviewees in your report.

Editing Log

Use this editing log or create a similar one of your own to keep track of the grammar errors that you make in your writing. By logging and correcting your errors, you will begin to see which errors you make the most. Once you recognize the grammar items that are the most problematic for you, editing becomes easier.

Error	Symbol	Original Sentence	Revised Sentence
Parallel Structure	//	My father's strength, wisdom, and determine have strongly influenced my life.	My father's strength, wisdom, and determination have strongly influenced my life.

APPENDIX 10 Correction Symbols

Your teacher may use symbols to indicate specific error types in your writing. The charts below include symbols, explanations, and sample sentences for some of these errors. You can use these symbols to help make the necessary corrections while you are editing your own work. The first chart refers to grammar items that are presented in *Eye on Editing 2*. For further explanation and practice, refer to the appropriate chapters or appendices in *Eye on Editing 2*. The second chart presents other common correction symbols.

CHART 1

Symbol	Meaning	Sample Sentence	Eye on Editing 2
cs	comma splice; using a comma to connect two sentences	cs It was a beautiful day, there wasn't a cloud in the sky.	Chapter 5
det	determiner error	det It is a most interesting book that I have read.	Chapter 3
frag	fragment; a partial sentence punctuated as a complete sentence	frag When we practice. The team must work together.	Chapters 7, 8
id	problem with idioms or set expressions	id We always agree to our teachers.	Appendices 5, 6, 7
num	noun error (number)	num We have enough homeworks to last a week.	Chapter 3
p	punctuation error	p I remember, graduation as the most memorable event.	Appendices 4, 8 Chapters 5, 6, 7, 8
ro	run on; two or more sentences without punctuation between them	ro The lecture was very interesting it went by so fast.	Chapter 5

(continued on next page)

CHART 1 *(continued)*

Symbol	Meaning	Sample Sentence	Eye on Editing 2
s-v	subject-verb agreement error	s-v She never <u>go</u> to the library to study.	Chapter 1 Appendix 3
t	verb tense error	t We <u>haven't completed</u> the project yesterday.	Chapter 1
vb	verb form error	vb They <u>haven't went</u> to the gym in weeks.	Chapters 1, 2, 4, 8 Appendix 2
wf	word form error	wf Her father is the most <u>success</u> software engineer in the firm.	Chapter 5
//	faulty parallelism	// We hoped for relaxation, peace and <u>to have good weather</u>.	Chapter 5

CHART 2

Symbol	Meaning	Sample Sentence
prn	pronoun error	prn My friend and <u>me</u> went to the movies.
ref	unclear pronoun reference	ref We enjoyed the book and the movie, but <u>it</u> was more violent.
sp	spelling error	sp My apartment is <u>noisey</u> and expensive.
ww	wrong word	ww He is the best offensive player <u>in</u> the team.
^	insert missing word	They are interested going with us to the concert. ^
ɣ	delete	ɣ His writing is clear, and concise, and interesting to read.
¶	paragraph	¶ This is the prominent theme. A secondary theme explains . . .
#	add a space	# My friends went to the club eventhough it's very expensive. ^
⟳	move here	The essay was interesting that we stayed up all night writing.
∿	transpose	We hardly could remember the way to your house.

APPENDIX 11   Grammar Book References

Eye on Editing 2	Understanding and Using English Grammar, Third Edition	Focus on Grammar, High-Intermediate, Second Edition	Grammar Express, First Edition
Chapter 1 Tenses and Time Shifts	**Chapter 1** Overview of Verb Tenses **Chapter 2** Present and Past, Simple, and Progressive, **Chapter 3** Perfect and Perfect Progressive Tenses **Chapter 4** Future Time **Chapter 5** Adverb Clauses of Time and Review of Verb Tenses	**Unit 1** Simple Present Tense and Present Progressive **Unit 2** Simple Past Tense and Past Progressive **Unit 3** Present Perfect, Present Perfect Progressive, and Simple Past Tense **Unit 4** Past Perfect and Past Perfect Progressive **Unit 5** Future and Future Progressive **Unit 6** Future Perfect and Future Perfect Progressive	**Unit 1** Present Progressive **Unit 2** Simple Present Tense **Unit 3** Non-Action Verbs **Unit 4** Present Progressive and Simple Present Tense **Unit 6** Simple Past Tense: Affirmative Statements **Unit 7** Simple Past Tense: Negative Statements and Questions **Unit 9** Past Progressive **Unit 10** Past Progressive and Simple Past Tense **Unit 11** Present Perfect: *Since* and *For* **Unit 12** Present Perfect *Already* and *Yet* **Unit 13** Present Perfect: Indefinite Past **Unit 14** Present Perfect and Simple Past Tense **Unit 15** Present Perfect Progressive **Unit 16** Present Perfect and Present Perfect Progressive **Unit 17** Past Perfect **Unit 18** Past Perfect Progressive **Unit 19** Future: *Be going to* and *Will* **Unit 20** Future: Contrast **Unit 21** Future Time Clauses **Unit 22** Future Progressive **Unit 23** Future Perfect and Future Perfect Progressive
Chapter 2 Modals	**Chapter 9** Modals, Part 1 **Chapter 10** Modals, Part 2	**Unit 15** Modals and Modal-Like Verbs: Review **Unit 16** Advisability and Obligation in the Past **Unit 17** Speculations and Conclusions about the Past	**Unit 27** Ability: *Can, Could, Be able to* **Unit 28** Permission: *May, Can, Could, Do you mind if . . . ?* **Unit 29** Requests: *Will, Can, Could, Would you mind if . . . ?* **Unit 30** Advice: *Should, Ought to, Had better* **Unit 31** Suggestions: *Could, Why don't . . . ? Why not . . . ?*

Eye on Editing 2	Understanding and Using English Grammar, Third Edition	Focus on Grammar, High-Intermediate, Second Edition	Grammar Express, First Edition
Chapter 2 (continued)			**Unit 32** Preferences: *Prefer, Would prefer, Would rather*
			Unit 33 Necessity: *Have (got) to* and *Must*
			Unit 34 Choice: *Don't have to;* No Choice: *Must not* and *Can't*
			Unit 35 Expectations: *Be supposed to*
			Unit 36 Future Possibility: *May, Might, Could*
			Unit 37 Assumptions: *May, Might, Could, Must, Have (got) to, Can't*
			Unit 38 Advisability in the Past: *Should have, Ought to have, Could have, Might have*
			Unit 39 Speculations about the Past: *May have, Might have, Can't have, Could have, Must have, Had to have*
Chapter 3 Nouns and Determiners	**Chapter 7** Nouns **Chapter 8** Pronouns		**Unit 56** Nouns **Unit 57** Quantifiers **Unit 58** Articles: Indefinite and Definite **Unit 59** Ø (No Article) and *The* **Unit 60** Reflexive Pronouns and Reciprocal Pronouns
Chapter 4 The Passive Voice	**Chapter 11** The Passive	**Unit 18** The Passive **Unit 19** The Passive with Modals and Modal-Like Expressions **Unit 20** The Passive Causative	**Unit 61** The Passive: Overview **Unit 62** The Passive with Modals **Unit 63** The Passive Causative
Chapter 5 Coordination and Parallel Structure	**Chapter 16** Coordinating Conjunctions		
Chapter 6 Adjective Clauses	**Chapter 13** Adjective Clauses	**Unit 13** Adjective Clauses with Subject Relative Pronouns **Unit 14** Adjective Clauses with Object Relative Pronouns or *When* and *Where*	**Unit 69** Adjective Clauses with Subject Relative Pronouns **Unit 70** Adjective Clauses with Object Relative Pronouns or *When* and *Where* **Unit 71** Adjective Clauses: Identifying and Non-Identifying

Eye on Editing 2	Understanding and Using English Grammar, Third Edition	Focus on Grammar, High-Intermediate, Second Edition	Grammar Express, First Edition
Chapter 7 Adverb Clauses	**Chapter 5** Adverb Clauses of Time and Review of Verb Tenses **Chapter 17** Adverb Clauses **Chapter 18** Reduction of Adverb Clauses to Modifying Adverbial Phrases **Chapter 19** Connectives that Express Cause and Effect, Contrast, and Condition		
Chapter 8 Condi-tionals	**Chapter 20** Conditional Sentences and Wishes	**Unit 21** Factual Conditionals: Present **Unit 22** Factual Conditionals: Future **Unit 23** Unreal Conditionals: Present **Unit 24** Unreal Conditionals: Past	**Unit 64** Factual Conditionals: Present **Unit 65** Factual Conditionals: Future **Unit 66** Unreal Conditionals: Present **Unit 67** Unreal Conditionals: Past **Unit 68** *Wish*: Present and Past
Chapter 9 Noun Clauses	**Chapter 12** Noun Clauses		
Chapter 10 Word Order	**Chapter 5** Noun Clauses 12-6, 12-7 **Appendix A-1, A-2, A-4** **Appendix B-1** **Appendix D-3**	**Unit 11** Phrasal Verbs: Review **Unit 12** Phrasal Verbs: Separable and Unseparable **Unit 25** Direct and Indirect Speech **Unit 26** Indirect Speech: Tense Changes **Unit 27** Indirect Instructions, Commands, Requests, and Invitations **Unit 28** Indirect Questions **Unit 29** Embedded Questions	**Unit 54** Phrasal Verbs: Inseparable **Unit 55** Phrasal Verbs: Separable **Unit 72** Direct and Indirect Speech: Imperatives **Unit 73** Indirect Speech: Statements (1) **Unit 74** Indirect Speech: Statements (2) **Unit 75** Indirect Questions **Unit 76** Embedded Questions

Answer Key

Chapter 1

PRETEST (page 1)
Possible answers:

1. was running
2. was
3. ✓
4. ✓
5. have seen
6. ✓
7. has not been feeling well
8. has taught
9. will have been working
10. ✓

SELF CHECK 1 (page 4)
Possible answers:

1. are
2. haven't sent
3. am taking
4. have been studying
5. has been going on

SELF CHECK 2 (page 6)

1. broke
2. was not
3. had never seen
4. was studying
5. had been shining

SELF CHECK 3 (page 8)
Possible answers:

1. are going to leave
2. will be
3. will wear
4. is going to be
5. will be remodeling

SELF CHECK 4 (page 10)

1. has performed
2. belong
3. felt
4. finished
5. have had

SELF CHECK 5 (page 11)
Possible answers:

1. spent
2. are driving
3. are planning/plan
4. are considering
5. will go

EDITING PRACTICE (pages 12–14)
Possible answers:

1
1. believe
2. ✓
3. read
4. ✓
5. will rain
6. ✓
7. ✓
8. will be writing
9. ✓
10. will be showing
11. ✓
12. has read

2
1. have become
2. are
3. have been fishing
4. was
5. used to like
6. find
7. have seen
8. are waiting
9. have spent
10. am going to fish

3
1. is
2. still surfaces
3. have heard
4. enter
5. seem
6. takes
7. arrives
8. ends
9. are becoming
10. will experience

4 It seems that many teenagers (**1**) **look** at driving as a right rather than as a privilege that they (**2**) **have to earn**. In order for these young adults to take this privilege more seriously, many states (**3**) **have** recently **changed** their laws so that it is harder for teens to be on the road. I believe this is important because I (**4**) **have seen** many dangerous incidents involving teenage drivers since I (**5**) **got** my license five years ago. I know that I was part of the problem when I was a new driver, and I (**6**) **was** in many near accidents due to my careless driving. However, I was lucky. In order to keep everyone safe on the road, I think that parents and lawmakers should prohibit people below the age of eighteen from driving at night, with friends, and on the freeways. Most unsafe driving (**7**) **seems** to occur when one of these factors is present. To make the restrictions easier on teens, some cities (**8**) **have been considering** improving their public transportation systems. Though it (**9**) **will be** difficult for rural areas with small populations to expand public transportation, the benefits will be worth the cost. Changes in laws and improvements in public transportation could make a difference in keeping drivers safe. These changes may make teenage drivers mad at first, but if the changes are implemented, everyone (**10**) **will be** more safe in the future.

APPENDIX 1: PRACTICE WITH AUTHENTIC LANGUAGE (page 108)

1. use
2. found
3. processes
4. led
5. viewed
6. viewed
7. showed
8. don't know
9. are forcing
10. have apparently missed

Chapter 2

PRETEST (page 15)
Possible answers:

1. ✓
2. could have finished
3. can write
4. might find
5. ✓
6. should have studied
7. ✓
8. can
9. ✓
10. cannot practice until

SELF CHECK 1 (page 17)

1. should have traveled
2. should be waiting
3. should not have written
4. could play
5. did not have to work

SELF CHECK 2 (page 20)
Possible answers:

1. is not supposed to eat
2. should have been
3. Will
4. could have been
5. had to complete

EDITING PRACTICE (pages 20–22)
Possible answers:

1
1. ✓
2. must have been
3. could see
4. ✓
5. can fix
6. should have taken
7. have to receive
8. ✓
9. was supposed to teach
10. ✓

2
1. may be
2. have
3. may not have worked
4. may not have learned
5. may teach
6. might not listen
7. can be
8. should begin
9. can learn

3
1. must have felt
2. could talk
3. must have been
4. would say
5. could say
6. might have
7. could turn
8. should not take

4 Many believe that a single event can change the course of someone's life. The event (**1**) **could** be large or small, but it can make such an impact that one's life is never the same again. This happened to Daniel Rudy Rutteiger, whose life story is told in the film *Rudy*. Rudy dreams of going to the University of Notre Dame and playing football, but Rudy is small and not highly academic, so his friends and family think he (**2**) **will have to be** satisfied as a steel worker like his father and his brothers. For years, Rudy puts aside his dream and works in the steel plant, until his best friend is killed in an industrial accident. Rudy reclaims his dream and goes to Notre Dame to play football. Rudy (**3**) **would never have gone** to Notre Dame, played football there, and been the subject of a major motion picture if this one life-changing event had not happened. Other people's lives (**4**) **may not change** as dramatically as Rudy's, but events such as learning to swim, learning a foreign language, or even learning to ride a motorcycle (**5**) **may impact** life in unforeseen ways.

Like Rudy, I (**6**) **was able to begin** college last fall. This was because of a move my parents made. At the time of the move, I didn't realize how different my life in the United States (**7**) **would be** because of this one event. I (**8**) **can speak** two languages, own my own car, and work in any field I choose due to this single event. I don't think most of us realize the importance that one choice (**9**) **can make** in life, but like Rudy's and my experiences show, one event (**10**) **can make** all the difference in the world.

APPENDIX 1: PRACTICE WITH AUTHENTIC LANGUAGE (page 109)
1. could carry
2. could ever have imagined
3. can sense
4. could
5. may be able
6. may exhibit
7. could be
8. would like
9. can be trained

Chapter 3

PRETEST (page 23)
Possible answers:
1. confidence
2. the same as
3. ✓
4. is
5. ✓
6. Oranges have
7. the trash
8. ✓
9. pictures
10. ✓

SELF CHECK 1 (page 26)
Possible answers:
1. some new computer equipment
2. The violence . . . is
3. cups of tea
4. an essay
5. Physics is . . .

SELF CHECK 2 (page 29)
Possible answers:
1. Doctors . . . their
2. The computer is
3. Hawks are birds of prey.
4. but I left the gift
5. Some of the homework assignments

SELF CHECK 3 (page 31)
1. every culture
2. little information
3. a few friends
4. six ounces
5. too many papers

SELF CHECK 4 (page 32)
1. This grammar
2. one's/your
3. their
4. That movie
5. these

EDITING PRACTICE (pages 32–35)

1
1. Discrimination
2. a good dictionary
3. ✓
4. ✓
5. the library
6. a few friends
7. a few dollars
8. desserts
9. the largest number
10. ✓
11. ✓
12. Because of the lie, . . .

2
1. the
2. the
3. my
4. Ø
5. the
6. Ø
7. Ø
8. many
9. type
10. Ø

3
1. these phrases
2. the place
3. this
4. importance
5. each stage
6. adolescence
7. their
8. This
9. of the tasks
10. history

4 One of the best (**1**) **aspects** of my college campus is its diversity. The faculty, staff, and (**2**) **students** come from all over the world. In fact, the faculty and students are recruited with a racial, economic, and gender balance in mind. Over the past few years, the computer science department has actively sought female faculty, and this has in turn increased the number of female students (**3**) **in the department**. Another (**4**) **way** the campus encourages and promotes (**5**) **diversity** is through the classes it offers. The humanities and social science departments have several classes that educate students about a variety of cultures, religions, and literature. These classes are some of (**6**) **the most** popular on campus and fill up quickly each (**7**) **semester**. As on all college campuses, there are a lot of clubs and student organizations at my school. These social groups encourage students from different groups to mix and get to know each other in informal and friendly (**8**) **settings**. A few (**9**) **groups** have cultural nights when their members present songs, dances, and food from different parts of the world. My friends and I especially enjoy tasting food from different regions. I believe that as the world gets smaller, the steps that my college campus is taking to promote diversity will help its students to understand and accept each other. Hopefully, these simple steps will make the world (**10**) **a** more peaceful place in the future.

APPENDIX 1: PRACTICE WITH AUTHENTIC LANGUAGE (page 110)

1. a
2. the
3. their
4. the other
5. animals
6. Few
7. Ø
8. Ø
9. animals
10. the
11. research
12. Ø
13. dolphins
14. researchers
15. Several
16. this
17. cohabitants

Chapter 4

PRETEST (page 36)

Possible answers:

1. is translated
2. ✓
3. ✓
4. should be sent
5. was taught
6. ✓
7. is being developed
8. ✓
9. was held
10. It always happens . . .

SELF CHECK (page 40)

Possible answers:

1. was transferred
2. existed
3. are written
4. will be given
5. hope to be accepted

EDITING PRACTICE (pages 41–43)

Possible answers:

1
1. ✓
2. is always served
3. need to be taken care of
4. belongs
5. ✓
6. are committed
7. ✓
8. were blown out
9. has risen
10. is often caused by
11. ✓
12. must be developed

2
1. are believed
2. are seen
3. are sought
4. can be presented
5. are still remembered
6. were held
7. are not allowed
8. will be remembered
9. happened
10. will be understood and not forgotten

3
1. have occurred
2. were built
3. were created
4. have been designated
5. cannot be developed
6. be remembered
7. happened
8. was hit
9. were killed
10. were injured
11. seemed
12. be planted

4 Watching television still seems to be the preferred leisure activity of many students. Even in the age of the Internet, video games, and various interactive media, students consistently mention television as the way they like to relax. After conducting my informal survey, I was both surprised and pleased by the results. I thought that the Internet (**1**) **would be given** as the most popular free-time activity; however, I was wrong. Television (**2**) **was listed** as the most popular leisure activity. Although much of the programming on TV is of low quality, the television shows that students watch are generally of high quality. Soap operas and "trash" TV (**3**) **appeared**

on some students' lists of favorite shows, but the majority listed educational programs. Some differences (**4**) **were found** between male and female TV viewers. The shows that (**5**) **are watched** by males tend to be sports competitions and scientific programming. The programs that (**6**) **are preferred** by females are the interview shows and historical documentaries. Both male and female students agreed that political and news shows do not hold their interest. I thought nationality might make a difference in viewing preferences, but program preferences (**7**) **were not affected** by this. Even though those surveyed (**8**) **belong** to different sex, age, and nationality groups, television viewing habits (**9**) **were found** to be almost universal. It is important to note, however, that this survey included only university students, and this may (**10**) **have affected** the results.

APPENDIX 1: PRACTICE WITH AUTHENTIC LANGUAGE (page 111)

1. will be shown
2. have been collected
3. will be featured
4. are presented
5. is being highlighted
6. makes
7. are being represented
8. had focused
9. goes
10. was created
11. are not attracted to
12. get used

Chapter 5

PRETEST (page 44)

1. The passage discusses the American value of independence, and it also points out other common values.
2. . . . negative, unfair, and unjust
3. ✓
4. Simon loves English literature, so he wants to take three English classes next semester.
5. Not only does smoking damage your lungs, but it also decreases bone density.
6. ✓

SELF CHECK 1 (page 48)

Possible answers:

1. We worked all night, but we didn't meet our deadline.
2. I finished the coffee, even though it was bitter.
3. My study group worked hard, so we finished the project early.
4. The lake was closed due to contamination, but people were still walking along the shoreline.
5. Neither my sister nor my parents are here.

SELF CHECK 2 (page 49)

1. Vicki has improved her writing by learning grammar rules and editing carefully.
2. Mrs. Lee is searching for a new job and moving to a new house at the same time.
3. My best friend is good at listening, thinking deeply about a problem, and giving good advice.
4. My roommate was neither anxious nor relaxed the night before her exams.
5. I will study either painting or sculpture.

EDITING PRACTICE (pages 49–53)

Possible answers:

1
1. ✓
2. The play is neither entertaining nor funny.
3. Unaffordable medical care keeps people away from the doctor, so they become sicker and medical costs increase.
4. ✓
5. Mr. Bustillo was very well prepared for the speech, but he didn't do a very good job.
6. ✓

7. ✓
8. Sissela loves science, so she is going to major in biology.
9. Children learn a lot from storytelling because life lessons are taught in an entertaining manner.
10. ✓
11. smiled
12. Next winter Nasim wants an unforgettable vacation like helicopter skiing in Canada or snow camping on a glacier in New Zealand.

1. or	6. for
2. and	7. so
3. and	8. or
4. but	9. so
5. or	10. or

1. Power is even evident when love is involved. Individuals behave against their will simply to please their loved ones.
2. Power is an interesting phenomenon that doesn't always have to be used in a negative way. It is an influence that people should use wisely.
3. I knew my parents had authority over me, but I didn't fully realize the influence of their love until it was time to select a college.
4. I had been working hard for four years in order to be accepted at a particular college, so I was thrilled when my acceptance letter arrived.
5. Although I had worked, dreamed, and hoped to attend my first choice university, I almost gave up that dream for my parents.
6. Their love was a strong influence over me, but I knew what I wanted.
7. Not only was I strong enough to stand up against their power, but I was also able to rationally explain my decision.
8. The various forms of power are interesting to observe and learn from.

People need to have their own personal space. Even though humans are social animals, they need a place where they can get away from others, feel safe, and (1) **be in charge**. This personal space may be a neighborhood, a home, (2) **a room, or even half of a room!** Our space is apparent to others because we personalize it. One of the reasons we feel secure in our space is because our personal possessions surround us. Studies show that people with more belongings around them feel more attached to a particular spot, and this is especially obvious in dormitories where personal space is at a minimum. Possessions mark (3) **both** where a person's territory ends and the next person's begins. Students bring personal items such as computers, pictures, stereos, and stuffed animals from home (4) **so** their new space will feel familiar to them. I have done this, too. I define my personal space (5) **and** help others know who I am by putting up posters of Michael Jordan. When people come into my room, they will see my love of basketball, (6) **and** that I admire Michael Jordan. Not only (7) **did** I **bring** my basketball posters, but I also have basketballs, basketball shoes, basketball jerseys, basketball magazines, and everything else related to basketball on my half of the dorm room. I brought all of these belongings from home, (8) **so** now I feel half of the dorm room is my own. This has helped me feel secure during my first months in a new environment. My roommate has personalized his side of the room by hooking up all his electronic equipment. His stereo, CDs, VCR, DVD player, and TV define his strong interest in technology. If we drive down any street or walk into any home, we can easily see the variety of ways in which people personalize their space (9), **but** this human need is even more obvious in the confined space of a dormitory room. We all like

to believe we are unique, (10) **but** we all share a universal trait that is surprisingly strong—all humans need a space that they can call their own.

APPENDIX 1: PRACTICE WITH AUTHENTIC LANGUAGE (page 113)

1. romance	6. prompting
2. so	7. but
3. watch	8. delight
4. and	9. or
5. France, Spain, and Tennessee	10. and

Chapter 6

PRETEST (page 54)

1. ✓
2. The book that I borrowed from the library is overdue.
3. ✓
4. Alan's father, who has a Ph.D. in chemical engineering, has high expectations for his son.
5. ✓
6. ✓
7. Countries that have earthquakes need strict building codes.
8. Dr. Kaufman, who teaches physiology, will retire soon.
9. The concert tickets that Carol and I bought are in my purse. /The concert tickets, which Carol and I bought, are in my purse.
10. ✓

SELF CHECK (page 59)

1. Professor Sims, who we had for economics, is very fair.
2. Samuel Clemens, who wrote *The Adventures of Huckleberry Finn,* used the penname Mark Twain.
3. begin
4. The interview that I had yesterday with the director of operations went very well.
5. His cousins went to a wedding ceremony that was on the beach at sunset.

EDITING PRACTICE (pages 59–62)

1. Thoa's father, who used to play college football, is coaching the high school team.
2. ✓
3. The bulbs that we planted last winter should bloom in the spring.
4. The ABC software company, whose president just resigned, is in financial trouble.
5. ✓
6. The 1992 demonstration is an example of the unrest that we are going to study in sociology.
7. Extremely competitive people who always want to win damage valuable friendships.
8. ✓
9. Galileo Galilei, who never left Italy, was nonetheless known around the world.
10. ✓
11. The Puerto Rican culture of the1950s, which Esmeralda Santiago writes about in *When I Was Puerto Rican,* has not changed significantly in the last decades.
12. ✓

1. that	6. Ø
2. who	7. Ø
3. when	8. who
4. which	9. that
5. that	10. that

3. However, the British influence, which emphasizes order and organization, can be seen . . .
4. Christmas trees, which originated in Germany, . . .
8. Spanish, which is the primary language in Puerto Rico, has been replaced . . .
10. who accepted this at the time
11. whose importance

 The object that I am looking at is a three dimensional rectangle, although sometimes this object can be the shape of a cube or a sphere. Five sides are made of glass (**1**) **that is clear,** and there is either a removable top or no top at all. One usually finds this object inside a house or office in a room (**2**) **where** people are likely to meet, such as the living room, family room, or kitchen. This object is not mobile. It often has a small motor that (**3**) **keeps** the environment inside the rectangle clean. Even with this motor, the object has to be cleaned every few weeks. Plants (**4**) **that help keep this object clean** may also be found inside of it. Next to the plants, there are sometimes figurines (**5**) **that are set in brightly colored rocks**. Both adults and children like this object. (**6**) **Some people who have stressful lives** find this object soothing and peaceful to look at. People (**7**) **who** have these objects usually love animals. Animals (**8**) **that live in fresh and salt water** use this object for a home. The animals (**9**) **that live in this object** make good pets for a person (**10**) **who is allergic to cats and dogs**. Do you know what this object is?

APPENDIX 1: PRACTICE WITH AUTHENTIC LANGUAGE (page 115)

1. were published
2. that
3. that
4. ,

5. boost
6. do not
7. is
8. who

Chapter 7

PRETEST (page 63)

Possible answers:

1. Although I found a parking space close to my classroom, I still didn't make it to class on time.
2. Even though it is difficult and expensive to travel to the Arctic Circle, it is worth the effort.
3. Although I studied for the quiz, I still received a low grade.
4. ✓
5. While we were studying at Kylie's house last night, her father fixed us dinner.
6. ✓
7. ✓
8. He still doesn't feel comfortable in the ocean, even though he has been swimming for many years.
9. ✓

SELF CHECK (page 67)

Possible answers:

1. Amy had such a good time at the party that she didn't want to leave.
2. Because Ana Marie was sick, she didn't come to the party.
3. Even though the pool is warm, we decided not to go swimming.
4. Mitchell has to graduate at the end of this year because he is running out of money for tuition.
5. Despite the fact that my sister has spent hours writing her essay, she received a failing grade on it.

EDITING PRACTICE (pages 68–70)

Possible answers:

1. Although the class didn't agree with the teacher's grading system, we had to abide by it.
2. Even though Jane doesn't like the sweater her grandmother gave her, she wears it often.
3. ✓
4. Since I live across the street from school, I eat all my meals on campus.
5. ✓
6. ✓
7. We read that book last semester because it was a requirement of the course.
8. Camille finished the project on time because she stayed up past midnight working on it.
9. Although the price of electricity is increasing, we continue to consume more and more of it.
10. ✓
11. Due to the fattening dorm food, Gilbert gained 10 pounds last semester.
12. I need to get some new keys because I lost mine.

1. so
2. Before
3. Ø
4. since
5. While

6. Since
7. because
8. due to the fact that
9. Wherever
10. so that

2. when
3. Ø
4. because
6. Due to the fact that
8. such small a number of people that . . .
10. Because language holds so much cultural significance, it is vital that all languages, no matter how small, are kept alive.

In the short story "The Catbird Seat," James Thurber, the author, uses humor to illustrate the war between the sexes. Mr. Martin and Mrs. Barrows are introduced at the beginning of the story, and we immediately see Mr. Martin's intense anger toward his coworker. Mr. Martin is a boring man who is used to a strict routine, (**1**) **while Mrs. Barrows is just the opposite.** Wherever Mrs. Barrows goes, change follows. Mr. Martin feels her main goal is to disrupt and ruin his life. (**2**) **Mrs. Barrows has a strong personality, and a battle between the two follows.** (**3**) **Though** Mrs. Barrows doesn't realize it, she has alienated herself from all of her coworkers, especially Mr. Martin. Mr. Martin is so upset that he decides his only option is to murder Mrs. Barrows. (**4**) **Before Mr. Martin decides to commit murder,** he has never broken his daily routine of work, dinner, and two glasses of milk before bed. Even though Mr. Martin's decision goes against his nature, (**5**) **he feels there is no other solution.** (**6**) **Unless he comes up with a better plan,** Mr. Martin is going to follow through with his murder scheme. Fortunately, the murder scheme fails, and Mr. Martin's new plan for getting rid of Mrs. Barrows is better than murder, (**7**) **although it is still not completely honest.** Mr. Martin feels that Mrs. Barrows is (**8**) **so** despicable that his actions are justified. Despite the fact that Mrs. Barrows is a difficult person, she has good intentions. Mr. Martin fails to see this side of her personality (**9**) **because he is so scared that his precious routine will be destroyed.** Mr. Martin's routine is restored as soon as Mrs. Barrows leaves the company. Overall, this is a humorous story, (**10**) **although it is a shame that in the classic battle between the sexes, strong women are so often portrayed in a negative light.**

APPENDIX 1: PRACTICE WITH AUTHENTIC LANGUAGE (page 116)

Possible answers:

1. after
2. When
3. When
4. were
5. moved
6. is
7. can sneak
8. don't use
9. Ø
10. because

Chapter 8

PRETEST (page 71)

1. If Joaquin buys a new car, he will get an SUV.
2. ✓
3. ✓
4. Studies show that if people exercise daily, they will feel better.
5. If the two variables are equal and show the result that is expected, the researchers will be happy.
6. I would volunteer at a homeless shelter if I had more time.
7. ✓
8. ✓
9. If I were you, I would move to Hawaii and live near the beach.
10. ✓

SELF CHECK (page 75)

1. If I drive to school, I will be on time for class.
2. She will also do some other things differently.
3. If Julie had been invited to go horseback riding after class yesterday, she would have gone.
4. If I were you, I would buy a new car.
5. If the sun had risen earlier, Mr. Gupta would have meditated on the beach this morning.

EDITING PRACTICE (pages 76–78)

1. It would hurt Rudy's feelings if his friends told secrets behind his back.
2. ✓
3. When I wait patiently, I get what I want.
4. . . . because he would have companionship.
5. Traditions are difficult to maintain if people don't keep their families together.
6. ✓
7. ✓
8. . . . would be happy and feel better about each other.
9. ✓
10. . . . she will hear a lot of songs that she knows.
11. ✓
12. ✓

2.
1. would focus
2. were
3. would mandate
4. would design
5. would be
6. would attract
7. had
8. will be
9. would not have
10. graduate

3.
4. would look back
5. had
10. affected
11. would have
15. will change

4. If you **(1) want** to save money and achieve some peace in your life, try planting a vegetable garden. Saving money and achieving peace are seemingly unrelated goals; however, both are surprisingly attainable by planting a garden. If you **(2) know** the price of seeds, you can understand how inexpensive it is to grow an entire vegetable garden yourself. If you have ever found joy in growing a plant, you will understand how it is possible to find peace in planting. If you **(3) have** a small plot of land, it will be easier to begin your garden; however, a lot of land isn't necessary. Even if all you have is a small patio with a few containers, you **(4) will** still succeed in growing vegetables if you do the following. First, it is important to have good soil. If you **(5) compost** your garbage, you already have the perfect fertilizer for your garden. If you don't, it is possible to find good fertilizers at any nursery. Next, it's time to decide which vegetables to plant. This depends on the time of year. If it **(6) is** the cool season, vegetables such as broccoli, lettuce, and onions will do well. Summer vegetables like tomatoes, cucumbers, and corn **(7) will** grow well if it's warmer. Depending on the plant, you may begin harvesting in as soon as four weeks. One downside to be aware of is pests. Whenever you **(8) plant** your vegetables, you will have to be aware of vegetable-eating bugs. Try planting a vegetable garden any time of year, and see what you save financially and gain spiritually. Hopefully, at some point in the future you will say to yourself, "If only I had known the benefits of a vegetable garden earlier, I **(9) would have saved** so much money and **(10) found** enjoyment so much sooner."

APPENDIX 1: PRACTICE WITH AUTHENTIC LANGUAGE (page 116)

See chapter 7 AK, page 150.

Chapter 9

PRETEST (page 79)

1. ✓
2. ✓
3. That whales migrate south to Mexico in the winter has created a tourist industry there.
4. Is Ramon at home? I don't know if Ramon is home.
5. We don't know what time it is.
6. It is necessary that Bo get home before midnight or her parents will be furious.
7. A nutritionist recommended that I eat less.
8. ✓
9. ✓
10. The teacher said that water freezes at 32° F.

SELF CHECK 1 (page 83)

1. Talal is wondering where his roommate is.
2. What we love to eat is Italian food.
3. What they traditionally do in Australia is have picnics or barbecues on big holidays.
4. Why Flight 109 is delayed cannot be explained.
5. It is important that Mr. Lee primarily use an English-only dictionary in class.

SELF CHECK 2 (page 86)

1. The receptionist told me that Professor Romy was not holding office hours today.
2. Your boss asked me what I had learned at the conference.
3. My roommate's father asked me why I wasn't in class.
4. At 8:00 this morning, the professor told the student to begin the exam then.
5. When we were at Pietro's house, he claimed that the mess there was unusual.

EDITING PRACTICE (pages 86–90)

1. Education prepares people for what they will face in the real world.
2. ✓
3. ✓

4. . . . that she keep her jewelry in a safe.
5. Alice forgot whether she had used oxygen or not in the experiment to get the current results.
6. . . . that he would be late for his next class.
7. ✓
8. . . . if she could catch the 6:35 train even thought it was almost 6:30.
9. The nurse said to the new mother that . . .
10. That the world population is causing environmental problems is troubling.
11. ✓
12. ✓
13. What she loves is Indian food.
14. . . . is an area of inquiry at the university.

1. How parents	7. That
2. when a boy's	8. that they are
3. when he starts	9. that
4. what parents	10. that one have
5. that their child	11. that
6. that	12. that

3. how mistakes can be erased
5. that juveniles should be given a second chance
8. that they would not have had the opportunity to excel in their home countries
9. How people chose to use their second chances
10. The truth is that many take advantage of a second chance

The famous generation gap between young people and their parents that was so apparent in the 1960s still exists today. It is said that the generation gap is a division between two generations, generally young people and their parents. When parents and children discover they have little in common, the gap has begun to form. Young people maintain that their parents don't understand them, worry too much, and restrict their freedom. The parents respond that their children don't respect them, watch too much television, and want too much freedom at an early age. In other words, what children and parents respect (1) **is** vastly different. (2) **What** the reasons are for this lack of understanding is hard to say, but there are a few theories.

In previous decades, parents have said that the generation gap developed from young people challenging their parent's old-fashioned ideals and beliefs; however, in the technological twenty-first century, old and young generations have said that they are separated by different skills and abilities. These challenges are true for all families, but for immigrant families the problem may be more serious. The older generation (3) **tells** its children that they have lost all sense of tradition and culture. (4) **What** the children learn to value in their new culture is not the same as (5) **what** their traditional parents value.

Children of earlier generations have sworn that they (6) **would** not let this happen in their families, yet the gap has continued to exist. That a lack of communication and respect is causing their children to drift farther and farther from them (7) **is** shocking to this generation of parents. In order to slow the formation of the generation gap, it is vital that a child (8) **listen** to his or her parents. In addition, counselors suggest that parents (9) **be** available to listen to their children at all times. Many families don't know (10) **whether or not** they will be able to heal the gap between the generations, but young people and their parents must still try.

APPENDIX 1: PRACTICE WITH AUTHENTIC LANGUAGE (page 118)

1. what they'd read
2. why
3. so many capable students are

4. that
5. what they need to do
6. what might have been
7. what's
8. where they stand
9. we teach
10. how involved parents are
11. how

Chapter 10

PRETEST (page 91)

Possible answers:

1. ✓
2. We get off the bus at the next stop.
3. He didn't tell me where the car is parked.
4. ✓
5. Italian ice cream is especially good.
6. ✓
7. Last Saturday George and Lance went to the video arcade all day.
8. The two-story brick house that is on the corner almost burned down last night.
9. The librarian is reading a story to the children.
10. ✓

SELF CHECK (page 97)

1. The new German racing cars are winning all of the races.
2. The teacher called on me to answer the question.
3. Three weeks ago, Norma and I took the placement exam.
4. The hotel needs to know when you will arrive.
5. They hiked to the top of the mountain last Saturday.

EDITING PRACTICE (pages 97–100)

Possible answers:

1. Do you know where the social science building is?
2. ✓
3. Most passengers get off the bus at the midtown stop.
4. Pierre loves the spicy Cajun shrimp.
5. The woman who lives next door has a Ph.D.
6. ✓
7. The professor gave a book to Jane.
8. ✓
9. Les asked me where we should meet on Friday night.
10. Pat and Candice are studying math in the library.
11. Rarely has Mr. Wedner been on time to an appointment.
12. ✓
13. Before the last class meeting, the professor and I discussed my course grade.
14. John's work at the university involves physics.

1. slightly more difficult
2. mixed populations
3. what their common values are
4. may not be easily observed
5. may not always be obvious
6. They might even be
7. a high social priority
8. that go against the mainstream culture should be suppressed
9. hold a society together
10. getting rid of divergent values

1. a traditional Chinese technique
2. many other aliments
3. acupuncture has rarely been used
4. get over pain

5. The depth of the insertion is also important.
6. to deliver electrical stimulation to the needles
7. There are approximately 800 . . .
8. how acupuncture works
9. would eagerly recommend
10. it to others

 Young men in many peaceful parts of the world must fulfill a military obligation before they are a certain age. Many fully support this requirement while others who live in peaceful countries wonder **(1) why this obligation is necessary.** It may seem like a burden **(2) for a government to impose this on young men.** In order to convince new recruits of the positive aspects of military life, the government must convey **(3) the military's importance to the young men.** However, many young men **(4) who don't support the idea of mandatory military requirements** still attempt to get out of the obligation. Even though many feel too much time is taken out of their young lives, **(5) rarely are young men** able to get **(6) out of their obligation.**

Although there are those who disagree with the mandatory military obligation, **(7) most citizens will completely** support this so-called "rite of passage." Some support it because they feel secure when their lives and country are protected **(8) everyday by citizens who come from all walks of life.** Another benefit is military service allows young men to take several years to learn about life and their interests. Most older men **(9) fondly remember their few years in the military as a time when they learned about themselves** and gained valuable experience that has helped them in their careers. Some even propose that countries without **(10) a mandatory military** obligation consider the benefits of this type of program. However, in this day and age, both young men and women must fulfill this obligation if it is going to be fair.

APPENDIX 1: PRACTICE WITH AUTHENTIC LANGUAGE (page 121)

1. the mail to her house
2. the newspaper to the door
3. empty garbage
4. white rubber
5. always runs
6. the folks along his route
7. which says in red cursive script, "Michael Wilson is the best."
8. just treat
9. what you do
10. really turn
11. suburban retirement

Chapter 11

Possible answers:

TENSES, MODALS, AND PASSIVE VOICE

It is interesting to see how unexpected life events **(1) cause** people to change and grow. My grandmother is a good example of someone who had unanticipated events change the course of her life and her outlook. She was born during World War I and **(2) was raised** in a traditional family where the father went to work and the mother **(3) stayed** home to take care of the children. She believed that her life **(4) would follow** the same course. She married early and had three children before the age of twenty-three. Unfortunately, one **(5) died** before his first birthday. World War II was the second unexpected event to change the life she had planned for herself. Her husband **(6) was sent** to Europe and killed in France. Before his death, my grandmother had taken evening courses at a local college. She eventually **(7) received** her master's in social work and worked

for the state for thirty years. Because her life didn't follow the path she had planned, she has become a flexible, open-minded person. Unlike many people her age, she accepts modern ideas about marriage, divorce, religion, and pregnancy. She knows from experience that life is unpredictable, and the world **(8) will continue** to move forward. From her I have learned that we **(9) should not be** too rigid or we **(10) will be disappointed** about the paths that our live take.

TENSES, COORDINATION, AND PARALLEL STRUCTURE

Should I live at home and commute to campus or should I move into the on-campus dormitory? This question runs through the minds of many students as they **(1) prepare** to enter college. There are definitely benefits to both living situations. Many parents encourage their children to live on-campus so that their children can experience the freedom, friendship, and the **(2) responsibility** of being on their own. Other parents might encourage living on-campus so that their children learn to fully appreciate home **(3) and** all of its comforts. On the other hand, many parents would prefer that their college-age children commute. This option costs less money, keeps children under the parents' control, and **(4) gives** students more time to study and less time to worry about cooking, cleaning, and laundry.

When I made this decision, there were several factors that **(5) influenced** me to live on campus rather than **(6) commute** from home. I knew one of the advantages **(7) would** be meeting other students easily. Other factors that influenced me were the convenience of not having to hunt for a parking space each morning and not having to wake up early only to sit in traffic. However, I have a good friend who lives very close to campus, **(8) so** he commutes every day. **(9) Not only does** he **have** breakfast prepared for him every morning, but he also has a lot of spending money because he isn't paying dorm fees. However, he has made fewer new friends, and he doesn't attend as many parties as I do. Overall, no living situation **(10) is** perfect. When students make decisions about where they will live the next year, they should realize there will be both positive and negative aspects to any choice they make.

MODALS, NOUNS, AND DETERMINERS

Good **(1) communication** skills are important, but I believe the most important of these skills is writing well. This skill seems to be necessary in all parts of modern life. With so **(2) much information** given in the written form, I find that I judge **(3) other people** by the way that they write. Clothing and speech **(4) may have conveyed** a first impression in the past, but in this day and age, writing may be the only contact we have with other people. I have recently learned the **(5) importance** of writing in the business world. I have gone on several job interviews and at each one, I was asked to write **(6) a** short essay. It's clear that employers are looking more and more for the ability to write well. Grammar is obviously important for students. When I was in high school, I didn't realize **(7) the** importance of grammar and my grades suffered because I **(8) couldn't** make myself clearly understood in writing. I learned the hard way about using good grammar and a clear concise writing style. **(9) The same** lessons can be applied when writing letters, sending email, and jotting down notes to family and friends. Because we may be evaluated by colleagues, peers, family, or friends on our written words, good **(10) grammar** and writing skills are necessary.

TENSES, PASSIVE VOICE, AND ADJECTIVE CLAUSES

In London, England, there are many activities and sights **(1) that are** educational as well as fun. Some fun, educational sites **(2) include** the British Museum, the National Gallery, and the

Tower of London. The British Museum, (3) **which** is one of the busiest tourist attractions in the city, has a vast and diverse collection that may require several days to see. At the National Gallery, some tours (4) **are guided** to help guests manage the sizable collection. Before it became a busy tourist attraction, the Tower of London (5) **had** a history that people today (6) **find** horrible yet fascinating. Some activities and sights in London that (7) **are** fun but also educational include wandering around Soho, shopping at a Sunday morning street market, and dining at one of the popular London restaurants. When one (8) **is** in a foreign country, it's always interesting to watch people (9) **who** have a different culture, language or outlook. Even though these activities (10) **are not considered** educational in the traditional sense, they teach us lessons that we would not learn if we stayed home.

 ## NOUNS, DETERMINERS, AND WORD ORDER

The Day of the Dead is (1) **an** important festival that is celebrated in Mexico and (2) **many** other Central and South American countries. It is (3) **a** time when people recognize the cycle of life and death. The original celebration was held during July or August during the Aztec month of Miccailhuitontli. In the post-conquest era, Spanish (4) **priests** moved (5) **the** holiday to coincide with (6) **the** Christian holiday All Hallows Eve, so now the Day of the Dead is observed on the first two days of November. The day's activities include visiting family gravesites, delivering flowers and religious amulets (7) **to these sites,** and enjoying a picnic with family and community members. There are (8) **two very important** points to remember about the Day of the Dead. First, it is a (9) **holiday with a complex history,** so its observance varies by region and by degree of urbanization. Second, it is not a sad occasion, but rather a time of festivities and joy. This celebration is (10) **especially important,** so even with modern influences, people have kept honoring past generations and will continue to do so for generations to come.

 ## COORDINATION, PARALLEL STRUCTURE, AND CONDITIONALS

All Isaac and Juliet can think about is vacation, even though they just graduated from college and started working three months ago. Both of them love their jobs, but they can't believe they won't have a vacation for another nine months. They said that if they had known the company's vacation policy before starting the job, they (1) **would have negotiated** for time off at six months rather than twelve. This (2) **would have made** their first summer without a vacation easier to bear. At this point, all they can do is dream of time off from work. If Isaac (3) **took** a vacation now, he would go to some remote location without any distractions from phones, faxes, or (4) **email.** He would hike, read, relax, and truly appreciate his few days away from work. Juliet, on the other hand, would travel to a place with a lot of people and excitement if she (5) **went** on a vacation. She (6) **would like** to go to a big city with shopping, fine dining, and (7) **dancing.** In reality, (8) **neither** Isaac **nor** Juliet has a vacation day in the near future. They tell their friends who are still in school to appreciate the generous amount of time off

they have as students, (9) **and** when their friends go on vacation, neither Isaac nor Juliet wants to hear about it! If Isaac and Juliet were back in school, they (10) **would relish** each and every day they were not in class. Neither of them realized the importance of vacations until three months ago.

 ## ADVERB CLAUSES AND CONDITIONALS

According to Michael Korda in his book *Success!,* "success is relative." In other words, what one person considers a success, another may consider a failure. To be successful, each of us has to define the word for ourselves (1) **so** that we know when we have achieved our goals. Korda goes on to say that not everyone wants to run a corporation or lead a country, and in fact it may be problematic to start with (2) **such** grand expectations that are bound to result in failure. In fact, this type of unattainable goal leads to laziness, because the goal is so far beyond one's capabilities. Korda suggests that (3) **when** we make a goal, the goal should be reasonably realistic. After we make a habit of succeeding with moderate goals (4), it's easier to go on to the larger ones. If one (5) **has made** success a habit, increasing the level of ambition is natural and realistic.

Although Michael Korda makes a good point about making success a habit, (6) **I believe** it is important to always dream big. If I had listened to his advice earlier, (7) **I might not have started** college. Because no one in my family had ever gone to college before, I didn't think I was capable of college either. However, I had teachers, counselors, and friends who encouraged me. (8) **Because of** their encouragement, I have just finished my second year at a university. If people asked me for advice on achieving success, I would tell them just the opposite of Korda's advice. I (9) **would encourage** them to define success in grand terms and to make the goals as big as possible.

 ## ADJECTIVE CLAUSES AND NOUN CLAUSES

In many ways, language and dress help define (1) **who we are** and provide the first impression (2) **that** people have of us. From language and dress, one may be able to tell the gender, age, and even culture of a total stranger. Language such as "chick" for girl, "dude" for boy, "cool" for good, and "fine" for attractive clearly identifies different generations. Not only does vocabulary distinguish teenagers from their parents, but the intonation or rhythm (3) **that** their sentences have also places them within a certain age group. Although males and females of the same age may use some of the same vocabulary and intonation, they are likely to choose different words and expressions. Culture also plays a role in the language we use. In Chinese society, it is common to ask if someone has eaten yet. This is a traditional greeting (4) **that** came from a time of poverty and starvation. In many western countries, this greeting would seem strange since the most common greeting in the west is simply to ask (5) **how a person is.** Similar to language, (6) **what** we wear also helps identify culture, age, or gender. The socks and shoes, skirt length, or pants style that (7) **one** chooses all give us important information. It is true that (8) **globalization is** making the world smaller, but the choices (9) **that are made** in language and dress still tell others a lot about us. It has been said that (10) **you can** tell a book by its cover.